Fairy Tales and the Kingdom of God
by
Allen Whitman

DOVE PUBLICATIONS
Pecos, New Mexico 87552

Author's Acknowledgements

My debt to the writings of C.G. Jung, J.R.R. Tolkien and C.S. Lewis is obvious to any reader. Not as evident is the help I derived from the *Apple Farm Papers* of Helen Luke on *The Lord of the Rings*; the insights of Robert Johnson, especially on the fairy tale, *The Spirit in the Bottle*; the thoughts of Rosemary Haughton and Walter Wink in their respective books, *Tales from Eternity* and *The Bible in Human Transformation*.

Publisher's Acknowledgements

Dove Publications is grateful to the following publishers for permission to use copyrighted material in this book:

A.M. Heath & Co., London, England, for an excerpt from *Tales from Eternity* by Rosemary Haughton, copyright © Rosemary Haughton.

Houghton Mifflin Company, Boston, MA, for excerpts from *The Lord of the Rings* by J.R.R. Tolkien. Copyrights ©1965 by J.R.R. Tolkien. Reprinted by permission of Houghton Mifflin Company. Also for permission to use an excerpt from *Tree and Leaf* by J.R.R. Tolkien, Copyright 1964 by George Allen and Unwin, Ltd. Reprinted by permission of Houghton Mifflin Company.

Macmillan Publishing Co., Inc., for excerpts from *The Lion, the Witch and the Wardrobe* by C.S. Lewis, copyright © 1950 by The Trustees of the Estate of C.S. Lewis and renewed in 1978 by Arthur Owen Barfield; for excerpts from *The Voyage of the Dawn Treader* by C.S. Lewis, copyright © 1952 by The Trustees of the Estate of C.S. Lewis and renewed 1980 by Arthur Owen Barfield; for excerpts from *The Magician's Nephew* by C.S. Lewis, copyright © 1955 by C.S. Lewis; for excerpts from *The Last Battle* by C.S. Lewis, copyright © 1956 by C.S. Lewis. Reprinted with permission of Macmillan Publishing Co., Inc.

Division of Christian Education of the National Council of the Churches of Christ, USA, for Scripture quotations from the *Revised Standard Version Common Bible*, copyrighted © 1973.

Western Publishing Company, Inc., for "The Emperor's New Clothes," "Rumpelstiltskin," "Snow White," "The Frog King," and "Hansel and Gretel" from *Fifty Famous Fairy Tales*, copyright 1954, 1946 by Western Publishing Company, Inc. Reprinted by permission.

COVER DESIGN: Margaret West

To Janet, who has no use for fairy stories

Table of Contents

Foreword

Few of us in the western world are easily touched by the Gospel message. So often we fail to feel its transforming power. There are many reasons for this state of affairs. We live in a materialistic world which has little place for the Kingdom of Heaven. We have been trained in a rationalistic, left-brain way of thinking which keeps us insulated from the stories and pictures which can bring us under the spell of the good news. We have received just enough of the Gospel to immunize us against truly being caught up in the incredible renewing presence of the Kingdom.

How can we break through this shell which our culture has built up around us? This is the question that Allen Whitman tackles in this engaging little book. Working as a counselor, lecturer and minister, he has discovered a method which has released many people from their immunity to the transforming power of the Kingdom of God. I have used a similar practice to help break up the ice jams in my own life. And I have discovered that other people can also use the imagination to open themselves to new life.

The author shows that fairy tales are a form of imagination which give us entry to the creative depth of our souls. These tales often express the basic Gospel message. They speak of release or escape from the problems and difficulties with which we cannot deal by ourselves, and they promise victory over these obstacles, with renewal and eternal life beyond them. These stories not only take evil very seriously, but even offer hints on how it can be

1

defeated. And best of all, when we let fairy tales write themselves through us, we share in this victory.

We should not be surprised that these natural productions of the soul or psyche are so close to the message and life of Christ. Tertullian reminds us that the soul is *naturally Christian*. And William Blake proclaims that the proper use of real imagination can take us into heaven itself.

Whitman first of all introduces us to an understanding of the language and meanings found in the fairy tale. Then he illustrates how easily we can pick up this language by guiding us through some of the well-known ancient tales. In the next section he leads us into the depth and significance of Tolkien's great trilogy with the best simple summary and explanation of this monumental work that I have encountered. Then he shows how C. S. Lewis gets around our western prejudices by using the same basic fairy tale mode in his Narnia stories.

Best of all, this book concludes with a section showing how we can write our own fairy tales and so step into the transforming process of which the Gospel speaks. Examples are provided of stories written by ordinary people who had never attempted this form of expression before. We have more gifts hidden in the secret place of our heart than we imagine.

I was so captivated by the flow of the material that I read the book through in one sitting — something rare for me. I will return to it again and again, and I shall continue to allow "the dreamer within" to spin out tales of the soul for me.

Morton Kelsey
Advent, 1982

Preface

Over the years, I have become interested both in fairy tales and in what Jesus meant by the Kingdom of God—the realm of God among us, within us and at hand. I enjoy the former; my everlasting destiny is tied up with the latter.

Lately I have become aware that there are connections and analogies between the two. *Not that the Kingdom of God is a fairy tale—far from it!* But rather that fairy tales can illuminate and bring a fresh perspective to our Lord's teaching about the Kingdom. In fact, fairy tales not only convey truths in folk art form, but the writing of such tales out of our own depth enables us to see traces of that reality towards which the term, "Kingdom of God," points.

The correlations between fairy tales and the Kingdom of God are sometimes actual, sometimes symbolic; but they are there:

1. The childlike attitude necessary to enjoy a fairy tale or to receive the Kingdom of God.

2. The fallibility of the hero/heroine of the fairy story—likewise the saints of the Church.

3. The other world of time and story in which the hearer of the fairy tale and the experiencer of the Kingdom find themselves.

4. The commitment necessary if the quest is to succeed—the Kingdom to be realized.

5. The inevitable conflicts with adversity and evil that beset one in the fairy tales and living in the Kingdom.

6. The Grace, the aid, the assistance that are and must be given if one is to win the prize, achieve the goal or grow within the Kingdom.

7. The final triumph over desperate circumstances — the happy ending common to both.

Like the quadrants of a compass, this little book is divided into four parts.

Part I Light thrown upon the Kingdom of God by short, familiar fairy tales.

Part II Our growth within the Kingdom reflected in J.R.R. Tolkien's *The Lord of the Rings*.

Part III The use of fairy tales by C.S. Lewis.

Part IV How the writing of your own fairy tales may bring you more deeply into the Kingdom itself.

Introduction

Any casual reading of the New Testament will indicate that the central reality to which our Lord points is what he calls "the Kingdom of God." "The time is fulfilled and the kingdom of God is at hand; repent, and believe in the gospel" (Mark 1:15).

What our Lord means by the term, "Kingdom of God," defies a simple explanation; for, as Norman Perrin has written, it is not so much a conception as a symbol for a reality and an experience. For this reason, Jesus uses his own actions as well as his parables to help us see and have some understanding of it.

At the very least, the Kingdom of God is the presence, the initiative, the activity of God in your life and mine, a non-physical reality intersecting with our sensory, historical world. It is manifested in our space-time existence when we do the will of God, as it is done in heaven. Nevertheless, having said this rationally, it is still true that the Kingdom of God is a mystery that can be known but never fully described or interpreted.

However, our Lord is clear that to enter the Kingdom of God, we must become as little children—open, trusting, receptive and believing. This is where fairy tales come in. As J.R.R. Tolkien puts it, fairy tales offer us a secondary world like the Kingdom of God which we believe in as long as we are in it. It is the child, the "kid" in us, which snaps at the bait, "Once upon a time, there lived in the great forest an elf . . ." which allows us to be drawn both into the fairy tale and into the Kingdom of God itself.

In other words, our attitude towards fairy tales and to the Kingdom of God must be similar. Moreover, fairy tales offer us an analogy to what Jesus means by the Kingdom because we can be caught up in the fairy story and be living in our own world all at the same time. This is true about God's Kingdom which is in us and among us, according to Jesus, if we have the eyes to see and the ears to understand.

Now as you may be aware, a fairy tale may or may not speak of fairies. Yet all such stories lead us into an arena of magic and enchantment inhabited not only by human beings but by other strange creatures such as elves, witches, goblins, talking animals and their ilk. Furthermore, according to Tolkien, they combine to a peculiar degree "fantasy, escape and recovery or consolation," making them strangely akin to the Christian Gospel itself.

Take fantasy, for example. Fantasy is a natural human activity that can be developed into an imaginative art out of which we build other worlds from the primal stuff of our earthly existence. In such a fashion, we can create symbolic models of invisible realities or values that otherwise we might deny or discount entirely. Yet, as Tolkien indicates, fantasy is based on reasoned facts. If we could not distinguish between frogs and Kings, the frog-King of the fairy tale would have no meaning for us. By the same token, when Jesus proclaims the Kingdom of God, he is speaking about something very concrete to him and assumes we have some idea of Kings and Kingdoms, not to mention some glimmering of what he signifies by "God."

According to Tolkien, we often view "escape" in a negative, pejorative sense of retreating from harsh realities into an illusory world of make-believe. But the Bible speaks of escape in a positive fashion; i.e., the escape from Egypt out of the house of bondage. Thus, one can be a prisoner of sin and escape into the freedom of whole new life, in Christ. The Gospels claim that this is indeed the way the Holy Spirit works.

The fairy tale offers this same positive conception of "escape." It is the nature of the tale that the hero discovers strange resources and allies that lead him out of desperate situations to succeed in his quest. Cinderella is released

6

from her oppression when she marries the handsome prince. Little Red Riding Hood escapes from the jaws of the hungry wolf. In so doing, the stories illustrate Paul's words that, in Christ, the whole creation will be set free from its bondage to sin and obtain the glorious liberty of the children of God (Rom. 8:21).

Thus there is in fairy tales a quality that Tolkien calls recovery and consolation. In fairy tales there is always triumph over tragedy. Tolkien coins another word, "eucatastrophe," to describe the happy ending. Cinderella's foot fits into the shoe held by the handsome Prince. They marry and live happily ever after. In this respect, fairy tales are not unlike the Gospels which end not with the crucifixion, but with Easter and the Resurrection.

Tolkien is not the only writer who has seen the correlations between fairy tales and the Biblical drama. Rosemary Haughton in her book, *Tales from Eternity*, offers another series of comparisons which again are helpful. Fairy stories, she notes, deal with powers and destinies over which the hero and heroine have little control, yet which are theirs to own and in which they have something to do. This is practically a description of Christian disciples following the Master, partially blind, and yet guided by the Holy Spirit.

Furthermore, she continues, the ethic of the fairy tale, to say the least, is eccentric—a far cry from the mores of the day. The hero may have to kill the fox that has aided him, use deception on the wicked witch, or boil another in oil. But then the Bible has some strange tales like Jacob cheating his brother, Esau; Abraham about to sacrifice his son, Isaac; or our Lord eating with publicans and sinners. Indeed, the early churchmen antagonized their brethren by relativizing the Jewish law and drew down upon themselves the wrath of the Roman authorities for disobeying their decrees on emperor worship.

Again, Mrs. Haughton points out that the hero of the fairy story, like you and me, is never pictured as an infallible being of high moral character, but a finite, limited kind of soul who invariably makes mistakes. The great virtues in the fairy tale are an openness to the resources available and a commitment to the task or quest. If this is not a fair

7

description of a Christian pilgrim, I don't know what is!

Finally, there is one other aspect of the fairy tale that brings it in line with the Gospels, a dimension that is often ignored. The fairy story takes evil seriously. Evil is personified in many forms — goblins, hideous animals with two heads, wicked witches and jealous relatives. But the work of the Evil One is given its due. There is nothing pollyannaish about a fairy story; in fact, for this reason many parents have wondered whether their little children should read such stories for fear of scaring them out of a day's growth.

Yet there is evil afloat, inside and outside of us. As the New Testament affirms, the Devil prowls among us as a roaring lion. To neglect the power of the Evil One is to make us unwittingly fall under his spell through unconsciousness on our part. A reader of the fairy story is made aware of evil even as is the student of Holy Scriptures.

Let me reiterate, I am not implying that the Kingdom of God is a fantasy, a mere figment of human imagination. Rather, I am using fairy tales to illuminate the inner and outer truth of the Gospels — to help them live.

Tolkien, a committed Christian, put it this way:

> Imagine the peculiar excitement and joy that one would feel if any specifically beautiful fairy story were found to be primarily true, its narrative to be history, without thereby losing the mythical and allegorical significance which it possessed.[1]

This is what he believed of the Gospel story, and I do too. The Gospels are narratives with historical content. They do not need to be de-mythologized; rather we the readers can understand them best when we use other tales to illustrate their depth.

PART I
FAMILIAR FAIRY TALES

Three Feathers

Once upon a time there was a King with three sons. Two were smart and clever, but the youngest didn't talk much, was rather simple and never was called anything but "Dumbkin." When the King became old and weak, he did not know which son should inherit his Kingdom, so he decided upon a test. The son who found the finest carpet and brought it back to him would become King after his death.

He told his sons he would release three feathers into the air. Each would go in the direction of a feather to look for the carpet that would win the Kingdom for him.

So the old King blew three feathers into the air. One went east, another west, but the third feather dropped right to the ground.

The older brothers took off after the first two feathers, leaving Dumbkin looking sadly at the feather lying on the ground before him. And there was nothing for him to do but sit and look down at his feather. Yet hardly had he done this, when Dumbkin noticed a trap door by his feather on the ground. Dumbkin opened it and followed some steps down into the inner room. And he heard a voice cry out:

Lady green and neat
Prunefeet
Prunefeet's puppy dog
Prune's here and everywhere
Quickly see who might be there

11

The voice was that of a fat toad surrounded by seven little toads. The fat toad asked what Dumbkin wanted. And finding that he was searching for a carpet, there and then he produced a finely woven one which Dumbkin then carried back to his father, the King.

Meanwhile, the clever older brothers had taken rough cloths from some peasants, so Dumbkin by rights had won the Kingdom. However, the first two brothers gave their father, the King, no peace and insisted on another trial since obviously Dumbkin was not fit to be a King. This time the King asked each to bring him a ring and again blew three feathers into the air. Just as happened before, one feather went east, another west, while Dumbkin's fell by the trap door on the ground. Just as before, Dumbkin was helped by the fat toad who opened a box and gave him a ring glittering with jewels. Since the older brothers returned with old wagon wheels, Dumbkin was again the winner of the trial.

But, as before, the older brothers insisted that Dumbkin could never rule, and the old King agreed to another test. This time the brothers were to bring back the most beautiful woman they could find. Again, the three feathers were blown in the air. Again, the older brothers went off east and west while Dumbkin followed the trap door into the ground. This time the fat toad put one of his little toads into a carrot pulled by six mice. But when Dumbkin brought them into the light of day, the little toad was transformed into a lovely woman, the carrot into a carriage, and the six mice into six handsome horses. The older brothers had settled on two homely peasant women, so Dumbkin had won again. And when in desperation the older brothers asked the King to let the winner be the woman who could jump through a hoop, Dumbkin's girl (who had been a toad) far surpassed the others. So it was that Dumbkin inherited the Kingdom, married the beautiful woman and then lived happily for many years.

■ ■ ■

How often in fairy tales it is the youngest in the family, like Cinderella, or the least likely one, who wins the prize, just as Dumbkin does in this tale. The same is true in the Gospel story. It is not the learned scribes or the moralistic Pharisees who discover the Kingdom of God through our Lord but naive, rather simple fishermen, folk from Galilee or sinners—a scraggly bunch at best. Rather than appear like Dumbkins, religious leaders looked askance at this carpenter from Galilee or secretly went to him by night, as did Nicodemus. For as Paul, the once-brilliant Pharisee, later put it, "Has not God made foolish the wisdom of the world?" (1 Cor. 1:20). And our Lord thanks his Heavenly Father for hiding the things of the Kingdom from the wise and understanding while revealing them to babes (Luke 10:20). In matters pertaining to the Kingdom of God, it sometimes helps to be a Dumbkin because then you start with no preconceived ideas.

Lest you have not identified yourself as a Christian Dumbkin, let me ask you how well you are doing the will of God, leading others into the Kingdom and becoming aware of the resources God is offering you. Or perhaps you're a little awed by those with a profound prayer life who quote Scripture easily and articulately witness to what God is doing in their lives. O.K., then you're a Dumbkin. But that may not be all bad. Maybe it's your brothers and sisters in Christ, charging off east or west, who have the greater problem looking good but getting nowhere. Remember, our Lord got far closer to stymied sinners than he did to churchmen who play-acted their religion to be acclaimed by men.

Possibly one clue from our story is that Dumbkin had to sit down before his feather and pay attention to what was right in front of him. This gave him a chance to go down into the earth, symbolically deep within himself. After all, our Lord did this when he went apart into the wilderness. So did St. Paul in the desert period following his vision of Christ on the Damascus road.

T.S. Eliot once wrote:
I said to my soul, be still and let the dark come upon
    you
Which shall be the darkness of God.[2]

Every sensitive Christian that I have known has had to struggle in his or her own solitude to discover dimly where God is leading. So it is not a mark against you to be a Dumbkin-Christian; it's where all true Christians begin and return time and time again. Seemingly that is the way God wants it. Only then do your resources open up before you.

One of the tantalizing aspects of our fairy tale is why the clever brothers should return with such inadequate offerings to the King's test when a whole Kingdom was at stake. Imagine bringing back old cloths for a carpet, wagon wheels for a ring and homely peasant girls for a potential princess or a queen. What was wrong with them?

The story doesn't tell us, but suggests that their own supposed cleverness got in their way. The fact is that they didn't take the King's trial seriously and totally under-rated Dumbkin who did.

They are somewhat reminiscent of all those church people in our Lord's parable who said they wanted to come to the banquet but then gave all sorts of good excuses for not doing so (Luke 13:18ff). It's like telling God, "Don't call me; I'll call you." Or perhaps the older brothers are more like those who think they can live the Christian life without any real commitment and discipleship—offering tips to God rather than real stewardship of their time, talent and energy, thus missing the Kingdom in and for themselves.

Several years ago I visited churches in the central African nation of Botswana. The land is poor. The country is largely the Kalahari desert. But I did see catechists or teachers traveling on foot or riding bicycles thirty miles to educate others in the faith. I did witness church schools competing with one another on Bible content, singing, and making their communities better places to live in. And it made me wonder about the affluent Christians in the United States who may never experience the Kingdom because they are so busy about matters of secondary importance. I for one grew up in a parish with many suppers, guilds and scouting programs—all good in themselves—but where I was never challenged to find and live in the Kingdom of God myself. I was never offered the opportunity of inheriting what Christ had left for me.

Dumbkin, however, a rightful heir, responded to the test. Here, indeed, is the good news. For in the words of Rosemary Haughton: "Each Christian is the youngest son, ill equipped, ignorant, liable to make hair-raising mistakes and to suffer for them, but upheld by the knowledge he (she) is sent."[3]

What is Christianity? Is it not the call to discover the Kingdom of God which is there before us and around us, and like sons and daughters of God, our King, realize our inheritance as did Dumbkin in this tale?

Jack and the Beanstalk

There was once a boy named Jack, the son of a poor widow. His mother had been married to a King, but a giant had killed the King and banished the Queen with her little boy from what had been their Kingdom.

Now Jack and his mother were very poor. And when all their money was gone, she sent Jack to sell their cow so that they could buy food for their table.

On the way to the market, Jack met a man with a sheep, who traded him the sheep for the cow. "It's far more valuable," the man told Jack. Farther along Jack encountered another man who swapped him his pig for the sheep. Then Jack traded the pig for a goose. Finally, he was hailed by a fast-talking salesman with whom he exchanged the goose for some brightly colored magic beans, which he took home to his mother.

When Jack's mother saw what he had brought home, she was so angry she threw the beans out of the window. During the night the beans sprouted, and grew and grew until they disappeared into the sky.

Being adventurous, Jack climbed the stalk, and at the top found himself in a strange, gloomy country. As far as he could see, there was not a tree or blade of grass, but in the distance he saw a great castle.

The castle was the home of the very same giant who had killed Jack's father. While Jack was watching, the giant came out sniffing the air and singing a song: "Fee, fie, foe, fum. I smell the blood of an Englishman."

Jack would have been in great trouble except for the

giant's wife. With her help, Jack took from the giant three treasures that had belonged to his father—a little red hen that laid golden eggs, a harp which played by itself, and a magic carpet that carried one anywhere one wished to go. When the giant chased Jack down the beanstalk, Jack chopped down the stalk with his axe, and the giant was killed.

At last Jack and his mother had all they needed. And they lived happily ever after.

■ ■ ■

At the age of fourteen I lost my father through a heart attack. Such an event in anyone's life can also mean you lose your faith and what relationship you have with God. Indeed, God may seem more like the evil giant than a benevolent Deity at times like this. It is no wonder that the tale tells us that Jack not only lost his Dad but the Kingdom as well.

So Jack and his mother are poverty-stricken. They are what the Gospels describe as "the poor in spirit" since the New Testament does not separate economic from spiritual destitution. If you have no money or food, you may well believe God has deserted you. If you have no personal relationships that are worthwhile, you are in the same depressing condition. The two seem to go together unless the person in that condition recognizes a need for God rather than becoming embittered. "Blessed are the poor in spirit," teaches our Lord, "for theirs is the kingdom of heaven" (Mt. 5:3). Those who acknowledge their spiritual impoverishment and are open to what Jesus has to offer are already one step into the Kingdom of God.

However, Jack, like most of us, does not begin by being aware of any "spiritual" need. He takes his mother's cow and starts wheeling and dealing. He trades the cow for a sheep, the sheep for a pig, the pig for a goose, the goose for a hen and finally the hen for a handful of beans. If you are rich in possessions and trade for pleasure, romance, travel, cars or drugs—without God—you end up in the same spiritual shape, namely with a handful of beans. For as St.

17

Augustine wrote centuries ago, you are rarely able to discover God until you're at the end of your rope. Only when the beans are cast out — only when you turn away from your ego-centered life-style and cast it from you, is the connection made within between heaven and earth. It is as though at that moment you are opened to a power greater than yourself and unconsciously something occurs — God and you are united. The discarded beans seem then to sprout into enormous stalks that disappear into the sky. It is the same psychic turning point that Jacob experienced in his dream of the ladder set up on the earth with its top reaching into heaven and the angels of God ascending and descending upon it (Gen. 28:12).

To Jack's amazement, when he climbs the stalks into the realm of the evil giant, he discovers positive elements there as well. There is the giant's wife, the little red hen who lays the golden eggs, a harp which plays by itself and a magic carpet than can take him anywhere he wishes to go.

From a naive point of view, all these possibilities are symbolic of God's Kingdom. There is the dangerous dimension of the spiritual life which you and I ignore at our own risk. "Fee, Fie, Foe, Fum, I smell the blood of an Englishman," roars the giant. God is not to be approached lightly or unconsciously, for as the Bible assures us, it is an awesome thing to fall into the hands of the living God. God's Kingdom is not to be toyed with or approached with anything less than full commitment. Our Lord reminds us that when we sweep our lives clean, we must be watchful lest seven spirits more evil than the first enter in, and our last state be worse than the first (Mt. 12:45).

In the Acts of the Apostles there is recorded the strange case of Ananias and his wife, Sapphira, both of whom collapse and die when their lies to the Church are exposed. Such deaths do not mean that God is vengeful but that you and I cannot turn away from honesty and holiness without consequences to ourselves. Paul is clear in his letters that immorality among Christians is self-destructive and endangers our inheritance of the Kingdom of God (Gal. 5:16).

On the other hand, there are other dimensions to the realm of God as well. The giant's wife protects Jack, enabling him to escape with the treasures that are there. Don't forget that Jesus tells us to ". . . seek first his kingdom and his righteousness, and all these things shall be yours as well" (Mt. 6:33). When the Kingdom of God is brought to earth, its energy and creativity can be translated into wealth (the little red hen) its music into the joy and harmony of friendships (the harp) while the magic carpet brings people and events into your life just at the right time. The moment we get our inner lives straight with God, outer circumstances change as well. The wrathful giant dies and what is left is the awesome love of God. The Old Testament is transformed into the New.

The tale ends with the familiar line that Jack and his mother lived happily ever after. I recall a *New Yorker* cartoon challenging such fairy tale conclusions. A father was reading to his young son perched upon his knee. The caption read, "And so they married and lived happily—for a time." But as a friend of mine once commented, "happiness" is what happens to you, good or bad; and true happiness is our ability to cope with either eventuality. This possibility, Jesus demonstrates so clearly, is a gift of the Kingdom itself.

The Emperor's Clothes

Long ago there lived an Emperor who loved new clothes more than anything else in the world. At any excuse he would show off his finery. His country was ruled by his ministers, while he spent his time before the mirror.

One day some clever men came to his palace claiming to be weavers. They told the Emperor that they could weave him clothes that could only be seen by the wise and honest and would be invisible to all who were stupid and unfit to govern the land.

The Emperor immediately put them to work. When he sent his ministers to see how the weavers were doing with his new clothes, they couldn't see anything. However, remembering that the fabric was invisible to those unfit to rule, they told the Emperor that everything was proceeding well.

The weavers, of course, continued to ask for more and more money to complete the costly garments. Finally, the Emperor himself with a few of his courtiers visited the weaving room. They saw only air but pretended the colors were simply beautiful.

The day came when the Emperor was to parade his new clothes before his admiring subjects. The weavers went through the motions of fitting the material over the King's body, pointing out that the fabric was as light as the shadows.

Then the procession began and the crowds looked at the strange sight — a naked Emperor strutting forth, followed by page-boys with a firm grip on an imaginary train of cloth flowing from the Emperor's shoulders. The people gasped, but recalled that the clothes were invisible to the stupid and ignorant. Suddenly a small boy cried, "Why, the Emperor is naked." The people began to laugh. The Emperor, however, shivering from a chill, held his head high and marched on, ignoring the tittering of the crowd.

■ ■ ■

Normally, you and I are duped, tricked or "taken in" in an area where we are particularly vulnerable to the deadly sins of pride, greed, lust, vanity, sloth, gluttony, aridity, etc.

I know a man who gave a comparative stranger a large amount of money to purchase diamonds because he desperately wanted to prove he could be a successful businessman. He was shortly shown to be the opposite when the diamond broker fled the country. No diamonds were ever produced, and my acquaintance was out a hundred thousand dollars.

Then there's the lonely man or woman who gets hooked into some marrying scheme by someone who only intends to fleece them. How could they be so gullible, we exclaim, only to fall into a similar trap ourselves in a different area of our life.

For this reason there is something embarrassingly painful as well as amusing in picturing the pretentious Emperor strutting down the street naked as a jaybird. Even his ministers and all the adults are afraid to appear stupid or unfit to rule by admitting the truth before their eyes.

There are some who think Christians are not much different from the Emperor, in the sense that they believe in an invisible God, follow an invisible risen Lord and claim to be filled by an invisible Holy Spirit.

Some years ago, Paul Van Buren quoted a parable told by the agnostic British philosopher, Anthony Flew.

Once upon a time, two explorers came upon a clearing in a jungle. In the clearing were growing many flowers and many weeds. One explorer says, "Some gardeners

21

must tend this plot." The other disagrees. "There is no gardener." So they pitch their tents and set a watch. No gardener is ever seen. "But perhaps he is an invisible gardener." So they set up a barbed wire fence. They electrify it. They patrol with blood hounds . . . But no shrieks ever suggest that some intruder has received a shock. No movement of the wire ever betrays an invisible climber. The blood hounds never give a cry. Yet the believer is still unconvinced. "But there is a gardener invisible, intangible, insensible to electric shocks, a gardener who has no scent and makes no sound, a gardener who comes secretly to look after the garden which he loves." At last the skeptic despairs, "But what is left of your original assertion? Just how does what you call an invisible, intangible, eternally elusive gardener differ from an imaginary gardener or even from no gardener at all?[4]

In short, the scoffers say that God is dead—the King is naked—the universe has no invisible clothes—that believers make up a god in their own image out of their own needs to make sense and give meaning to their lives.

Except. . . except that many Christians seem to have a power and a vitality that can be impressive when it's not "put on." And it's a funny thing, you remember those weavers in our tale who said their cloth could only be seen by those who were not stupid and unfit to rule? By implication, those who could see what they were weaving had a knowledge and a wisdom that others did not have. Well, maybe in the Christian view of things, those scalawags had a point. Because if J. B. Phillips is correct in stating that faith is a kind of intuitive x-faculty that puts one in touch with things invisible, a discernment of the Holy Spirit that comes when one believes in the risen Lord and follows him, then Christians are in touch with Reality in another way and have, as the writer of Hebrews explains it, "the conviction of things not seen" (Heb. 11:1).

But who wants to be out strutting naked before God? And who wants to find out for himself Christ is Lord? And who wants his life transformed? Who wants to look idiotic before the world? Who wants to risk the experiment of faith and wear the invisible robes of the Heavenly King?

Rumpelstiltskin

In a certain Kingdom there lived a poor miller who had a very beautiful and clever daughter. The miller was so vain and proud of her that he told the King that his daughter could spin gold from straw.

Unfortunately, the King was very greedy, so he ordered the girl brought before him and commanded her to spin gold out of a whole room filled with straw. "All this must be spun before morning," he told her," or you will forfeit your life." The poor girl cried that she couldn't do such a thing but to no avail.

Overcome and weeping, the girl sat down and looked hopelessly at the straw when suddenly a droll little man opened the locked door and offered to spin the straw into gold if the girl would give him her necklace. And, sure enough, in a very short time he sat down at the wheel and spun the straw into gold.

When the King saw the gold, he was very pleased and ordered the girl to spin more. Again the little man came through the door. This time he asked for the girl's ring before he went to work.

The next morning the King was delighted at his increase in treasure and told the girl that if she would spin again he would marry her. When the little man came this time, however, the girl had nothing to offer him.

"Promise me your first-born child," he said, "and I will fill this room with gold." The miller's daughter had no choice, so the little man did his work.

When the King saw the room filled with gold, he married the girl and made her his Queen. And by the time the Queen delivered her first child, she had forgotten about the strange little man and her promise. However, one day he came into her room and reminded her of it. She was beside herself with grief and begged him to release her, offering him all the treasures in the Kingdom.

"I'll give you three days," the man said, relenting slightly. "If you can tell me my name at the end of that time, you can keep your child."

The Queen hurriedly sent out messengers all over the land to discover the name of the little man. And on the third day one came back with a strange report. "Yesterday," he said, "as I was climbing a high hill where the fox and the hare bid each other good night, I saw a little hut before which a fire burned. Around the fire a funny man danced on one leg and sang:

> Today I brew, and then I'll bake,
> Tomorrow the Queen's child I'll take;
> The Queen will never win this game,
> For Rumpelstiltskin is my name.

When the little man returned, he asked the Queen for his name.

"Is it John?" she asked.

"No."

"Is it Tom?"

"No."

"Is it Rumpelstiltskin?"

"The witches told you, the witches told you," shrieked the little man. He rushed out and was never seen again.

■ ■ ■

There was a legendary Jewish rabbi who was named Bar Shem Tov—"The Master of the Good Name"—because he had the ability to use the right word or words to describe a person, thing or situation. This capacity gave him remarkable power and influence over those around him, for we tend to respect someone who with a word brings order

24

out of chaos, calms troubled waters, punctures the pretensions of a snob or clarifies a confusing issue.

Many scientists in our day have in another way become masters of the good name as well. When Einstein discovered that the energy of any particle of matter is equal to its mass times the square of the velocity of light ($E = Mc^2$), he not only made it possible to calculate the potential in a chunk of coal but set the stage for releasing the energy in an atom of uranium. For if man can name the way things work in nature, man has the ability to harness nature to his own ends.

However, no one was master of the good name more than Jesus of Nazareth. In his case, the whole Spirit of God was behind his words. As John in his Gospel reminds us, Jesus "knew what was in the heart of man," so his words unerringly hit the target. With this power, he quieted a storm, drove out demons, healed the sick, cleansed the lepers, and even brought Lazarus back from the dead. In so doing, Jesus demonstrated what God had in mind when God gave Adam the authority to name the animals and every living thing. "Naming," in the Biblical sense, means not only gaining power over another but literally calling a person or thing into being, filling them with life, purpose and direction.

I don't know if you have read C.S. Lewis' fairy tale, *The Magician's Nephew*. In it, two children, Polly and Digory, witness Aslan the Lion (the Christ figure) create Narnia with a song. The Lion sings and the music creates what he has in mind.

> Polly was finding the song more and more interesting because she thought she was beginning to see the connection between the music and the things that were happening. When a line of dark firs sprang up on a ridge about a hundred yards away she felt that they were connected with a series of deep, prolonged notes which the Lion had sung a second before. And when he burst into a rapid series of lighter notes she was not surprised to see primroses suddenly appearing in every direction.[5]

This is "naming" in its highest, most ultimate dimension. The song becomes the vehicle for the creative wisdom of God. With the Holy Spirit behind it, naming creates and transforms. You and I have the same power to a greater or lesser degree, for we are made in the image of God. A blessing can establish a relationship. A curse may destroy it. What happens depends on how strongly the Spirit and intelligence of God are in our words.

Now all this may seem far removed from the Queen's discovery that the little man was none other than Rumpelstiltskin. On the surface, it would seem she had merely solved the puzzle which absolved her of her promise. But the Queen's influence over the little man may reveal that Rumpelstiltskin was not just his "calling" name but his "true" name. The ancient world and many primitive cultures distinguish between the two. To have others' "calling" name enables you to get their attention and to speak with them directly, but to have their "true" name gives you access to their very soul. True names were therefore kept secret for fear that another might have undue power over you.

In the Bible, God has some calling names such as Yahweh or Elohim. When Moses stood before the burning bush and asked God for a name to give his people, the reply was I AM THAT I AM. God is. Yet this is still not God's true name, which is a mystery. For to have God's real name would mean that man would have power over God.

It is here you discover in the New Testament one of the most incredible promises ever imagined. Jesus Christ, whose names mean Saviour and Lord—not just his calling but true names—tells his disciples that they may ask anything in his name and the Heavenly Father will honor it. Glenn Clark has called this the greatest blank check in history. Jesus gives us his true name just as the waitress and secretary give us their calling name in order to serve us. By giving us his true name, our Lord has made it possible for us to lay our ordinary needs and concerns instantly before the Heavenly Throne.

However, this does not mean you and I can manipulate God or by magically intoning the name of Jesus use it as a talisman to protect us or have our own way. For centuries Christians have tried this, and it does not work. But it does mean that, relying on the name of Jesus Christ, we can be ushered into the Kingdom of God and be placed in a position where God's will may be done in and through us. When this occurs, when we are brought before God unto whom all hearts are open and all desires known, when God's Spirit begins to transform our lives, we are changed and so are our names. Thus when Jacob (whose name signifies "supplanter," for he had cheated Esau out of his birthright and father's blessing) wrestles with God at the ford of Jabbok, his name is changed to "Israel"—one who has persevered or striven with God.

Such reflections provide a handle for one of the most enigmatic statements found in the Book of Revelation. You will recall that John the Elder writes the Church in Pergamum that they have held fast to their faith and not denied their Lord during a period of persecution. And his message concludes, "To him who conquers . . . I will give him a white stone, with a new name written on the stone which no one knows except him who receives it" (Rev. 2:17).

Clearly, those who have remained faithful to Christ have a new, true name—their character has changed. It is like our Lord telling Simon that he will from now on be Peter, the Rock Man, upon whom he will build his Church. Through their suffering and closeness to the risen Lord, the Christians in Pergamum have been transformed like Jacob wrestling with God.

And this raises the implicit question of our fairy tale and of your life in Christ. What is your true name?

In our fairy tale, the little man who turned straw into gold turned out to be Rumpelstiltskin. In your encounter with God through the name of Jesus Christ, by what name are you now called? What is your new name and true name? Can you guess?

I for one can't wait to discover who I've come to be.

Snow White

One day long ago a lovely baby girl whose skin was as white as snow, whose lips were red as blood and whose hair was black as ebony, was born to a Queen in a far-off land. The mother named the child Snow White. Unfortunately, the Queen became ill and died. The next year the King, Snow White's father, married another woman who was beautiful but very vain and selfish. Her greatest treasure was a magic mirror of which she used to ask:

Mirror, mirror on the wall,
Who is fairest of them all?

And the mirror would answer:

The magic mirror tells you true,
The fairest in the land is you.

At least this is the way the mirror answered until Snow White was seven years old. Then the mirror replied to the Queen:

The magic mirror tells you true,
Snow White is lovelier than you.

The Queen turned pale with rage at this and ordered a huntsman to take Snow White into the woods and kill her. But the hunter was so taken by the beauty of the child that he left her in the forest and did not kill her. Happily, Snow

White came upon a cottage inhabited by seven dwarves who cared for her, allowing her to mind their home while they went out to work. Each day, they warned Snow White to be careful to let no one in the house because they knew one day the wicked Queen with her magic mirror would discover that Snow White was alive.

Sure enough, the Queen went to her looking glass and asked the question, "Who is fairest of them all?" The glass replied:

> The magic mirror tells you true,
> Snow White is lovelier than you.
> She's living still in forest glen,
> And dwells with seven little men.

The Queen was livid with anger and, disguising herself as an old woman, went to the home in the woods where Snow White was staying. She had prepared an apple, one side of which was poisoned, and offered the fruit to Snow White. When Snow White hesitated, the Queen divided the apple in half and ate her portion to show Snow White that nothing was wrong. But when Snow White tasted her poisoned half, she fell down upon the floor. And when the dwarves returned that night they thought she was dead and were not able to revive her. However, she looked so life-like they put her in a glass coffin so they might still gaze upon her.

Snow White lay like this for a long, long time, looking as if she were asleep. At last a Prince came through the woods and seeing Snow White immediately fell in love with her. When he lifted the lid of the coffin, the poisoned apple fell out of her mouth, and she awoke. The Prince took her to his father's palace and asked Snow White to marry him. A wedding was prepared and many were invited, including the wicked Queen. As the Queen was dressing for the marriage feast, she again looked into the mirror and asked the question which was always on her mind. The mirror answered:

> The magic mirror tells you true,
> The bride is lovelier than you.

When the wicked Queen heard this, she rushed out to see the new bride, and discovering it was indeed Snow White, she choked with passion, fell into a fit and died. But Snow White and her Prince lived happily ever after.

■ ■ ■

While you and I in Christ may be Kings and Queens in the Kingdom of God, both Scripture and fairy tales remind us that we can fall away from the Kingdom, frustrate its grace and even lose it. Thus, when the Queen stepmother in our fairy tale let her jealousy open the door for the evil spirit, she eventually lost her reign. This is also the very possibility Paul raises with the Christians in Corinth when he writes: "For while there is jealousy and strife among you, are you not of the flesh, and behaving like ordinary men?" (1 Cor. 3:3).

The English word for "jealousy" comes from the Greek, meaning "to boil." In the Hebrew language, the image is of one "being turned red in the face." So when you begin to boil inside and your face changes to crimson, it may not be anger or embarrassment but jealousy raising its ugly head. At that moment you and I are in the same spiritual danger as the Queen stepmother when she looked into her magic mirror which declared that Snow White was more beautiful than she.

I suspect everyone can recall when feelings of jealousy welled up within. During my high school years, there was a boy named Stan, slightly older than myself, who was not only tall and handsome but could glide across the dance floor with grace and ease. He always had the best-looking girl firmly in his arms. I don't remember my face burning, but inside I seethed with envy.

A woman friend of mine tells of watching a particularly fetching female teeing off for her drive down the fairway. "I hope she dubs it," she muttered to a companion, for no other reason than she thought the woman looked more charming than she did. None of us likes rivals.

Now you and I cannot help having such feelings, but woe betide us when we allow an evil spirit to start flowing through us so that we begin to gossip and do malicious things as a result of our jealousy. It can start a chain of events that takes us right out of the Kingdom of God.

Saul, a strong, tall, courageous man of the tribe of Benjamin, was chosen by God and anointed by Samuel to be the first King over Israel. But he let his emotions run away with him. He became furious when he heard some women singing:

> Saul has slain his thousands,
> and David his ten thousands. (1 Sam. 18:7)

Until that time, David, the young son of Jesse, had been his loyal supporter and the best friend of his son, Jonathan. Yet Saul became so frantic with envy that he threw his spear at David, intending to kill him. From that moment on, Saul rapidly turned away from the grace of God that had been with him as he ruled over Israel.

A dramatic illustration of jealousy in the New Testament involved the reaction of King Herod to the news carried by the Wise Men that a child was born in his realm who was to become King of the Jews. In his rage that anyone might supplant him, Herod had all the male children in and around Bethlehem murdered so that there could be no living claimant to his throne.

Unfortunately, this dark deed surrounding the birth of Jesus is rarely emphasized. The Feast of the Holy Innocents in the Church calendar is generally ignored during the Christmas season. Yet the fact remains that religious people open to the providential action of God may still either fall victim to evil from within or cause it to come down upon themselves and others from without.

Moreover, it does not help if we are like Snow White, pure and blameless. Unconsciousness is no virtue in Holy Scripture. When I was a boy, my mother gave me those familiar monkeys with their hands over their eyes, their ears and their mouths. I was to see no evil, speak no evil, hear no evil. However, if either I or a Snow White deny the existence of evil, then we may become its prey.

Jesus tells us that we are to be "wise as serpents and

innocent as doves" (Mt. 10:16). He is suggesting that we need the earthly wisdom of the dwarves, who were quite alert to Snow White's danger, while we are harmless as doves in self-defense. The Christian stance towards evil is to be conscious of it, confront it and yet refrain from becoming evil in return. We are to pray for our enemies, do good to them who hurt us and despitefully use us (Mt. 5:44). Thus it is the steadfast love of the dwarves and the emotional love of the Prince that redeems Snow White from her desperate situation—not any revengeful action on their part. The unrepentant stepmother suffers her own fate.

C.S. Lewis has pointed out that sophisticated Christians have dressed the Devil up in a pair of red tights and then ridiculed anyone who believed that he existed as an independent power. While the same people are fascinated by evil in movies, television, newspapers and books, they think it is absurd that serious Christians might encounter the demonic in the spiritual realm. But committed religious persons are just the ones who may become as possessed by the Evil One as Snow White's stepmother.

Take Paul for instance. In his letter to the Galatians, he writes that he was so zealous for the traditions of his fathers that he persecuted the Church of God and violently tried to destroy it (Gal. 1:13, 14). It took his encounter with the risen Christ on the road to Damascus to show him how blind he had been. Happily, the Christians in Damascus did not treat his as he had intended to deal with them. Instead of letting him rot away in his blindness, remorse and agony, Ananias, a Christian in Damascus, went to Paul, laid his hands upon him praying that he would regain his sight and be filled with the Holy Spirit. In so doing, Ananias won over to Christianity the greatest missionary who ever lived. The Evil One in Paul has been overcome. At the same time, no Christian in Damascus had been won over to Satan in the process. Moreover, Paul never forgot. A devoutly religious man like himself had been infiltrated by the demonic, and though he preached to others, he always reminded his hearers that he, Paul, still might become a castaway (1 Cor. 9:27).

Significantly, the Old Testament speaks of Yahweh as a

"jealous" God. We must carefully distinguish here between being jealous *for* someone from being jealous *of* them. The God of Israel is jealous *for* his people — cares for their well-being like a parent for a child. Human problems arise when you or I become jealous *of* another rather than *for* them. Since we are all likely to be jealous *of* another's abilities, looks, friends, money, social standing or career, the question is what you and I decide to do about such feelings lest they get the better of us. Will we let Christ enter our hearts at these moments or make space for an evil spirit? The Queen in our tale let the Devil in and eventually lost her Kingdom.

However, be of good cheer — Christians have the gift of a wonderful mirror into which they may gaze and ask their most pressing questions (James 1:23-25). We can look in our imagination into the face of Jesus Christ, our risen Lord, and inquire:

Mirror, mirror on the wall,
Whom does God love most of all?

I did, and do you know what the mirror replied?

Mirror, mirror tells you true,
God loves his Son who lives in you.

The Frog King

One evening a beautiful young Princess went into a wood and sat down beside a cool spring. She had her favorite plaything with her—a golden ball. She amused herself by tossing it against a tree and catching it as it bounced back.

After a time, she threw the ball so hard that it bounced by her and fell into the spring. Then the Princess wept as if her heart were broken.

Suddenly a frog popped up out of the water and offered to get her ball, but only if she would love him, let him eat from her golden plate and sleep with her in her bed.

Ugh, thought the Princess. I can't stand that slimy thing. But she wanted the ball very much and so she agreed. "Yes, yes, I promise. Only bring me my ball," she told the frog.

The frog dived deep into the water and retrieved the ball. The Princess snatched up the ball and ran as fast as she could back home, with the frog crying out to her to wait for him.

That night as the Princess sat down to dinner, there was a strange thump, thump at the door, and a voice called out:

Open the door, my Princess dear,
Open it for your lover, here.
Remember the promise you gave to me
As you played with your ball 'neath the old oak
 tree.

The Princess ran to the door and there was the frog. She slammed the door, but the King, her father, demanded to know what had frightened her. When she told him about the frog and her golden ball he told her, "If you have made a promise, you must keep it."

The Princess pouted but let the frog in to eat at her table and later carried him into her bed.

When morning came, the frog hopped out of the house to the Princess' great relief. However, that night the frog returned and insisted upon being treated in the same fashion. The third night he did the same, but before she went to sleep the frog insisted that he kiss her good-night.

When the Princess awoke, there beside her bed stood a handsome Prince with the most beautiful eyes she had ever seen.

"You," she faltered, "are the frog?"

"Yes," answered the Prince. "I was enchanted by a wicked witch and forced to remain a frog until some Princess should let me eat at her plate, sleep in her bed and kiss her. You have broken the spell. Now I have nothing to wish for but that you will be my bride and go to my father's Kingdom with me."

In a short time the Princess gave her consent and they lived happily many years.

■ ■ ■

When I was in the army, a wandering entertainer gave us another version of this familiar story.

Once upon a time, there was a beautiful girl who was walking along when she heard a voice calling her. Looking down she saw a little green frog. "What do you want, little green frog?" the girl said. "I was enchanted by a very bad witch," replied the frog. "And the only way I can regain my old form is for some lovely girl to take me home and sleep with me under her pillow."

Well, the beautiful girl was very kind-hearted. She

picked up the little green frog, took him home and slept with him under her pillow. Sure enough, the next day there beside her lay a handsome Prince.

And do you know, to this day her mother doesn't believe that story.

So you can see that this same tale can be interpreted at a variety of levels. However, if you read this story as illustrating one way you and I may be drawn into a new dimension of the Kingdom of God, then the tale takes on fresh significance.

The story begins with the loss of the Princess' golden ball. For untold centuries, a ball like the sun has been a common symbol for God. Indeed, according to C.G. Jung, the ball or sphere appears in our dreams as a figure of the Self, the God within. If such associations are appropriate and true, the Princess has experienced outwardly a loss of God or life and, inwardly, a diminution of Self.

Since you and I are psychosomatic unities, it is impossible for us to lose physical energy, friends or creative capacity without this affecting our relationship with God. Thus, persons who are miserably sick may interpret their illness as God's judgment upon them. Conversely, when we are "born again" through discovering God, we experience enhanced life and renewed energy.

Obviously, you and I may have lost our golden ball and had it retrieved countless times, yet have been unaware of its theological implications.

Nevertheless, there are certain matters about which we may feel such deep concern as to bring God into our reflections. As a young adult, I lost my "beloved" to another man and would have promised the frog anything to bring her back. Others have felt the same thing about their health, a job, or a place on the team. Serving in the infantry in World War II, I made all sorts of agreements with God if only I could return home in one piece, promises which I quickly repressed, as did the Princess in our tale, once the danger was over.

Like the Princess, we all want to have our golden ball returned without making any changes in ourselves. However, where a new attitude, a new maturity, is called for, the frog as a bringer of our wholeness will not let us off the hook. Our frog will begin to pound on our door and demand that we feed him, sleep with him, accept him as we promised.

In our story, it is the father who firmly tells his daughter that she must honor her word to the frog, detestable as it may seem. It would seem that our highest nature knows when such a thing is being demanded of us.

I once had a dream that a football coach was insisting that I lay off liquor if I was to play on his team. Although I'm no alcoholic, it was a time for discipline, for an act of the will on my part. The word "diet" means "way of life." The great problem of dieting is that our way of life may change temporarily, but then we return to old patterns of eating and behavior. Conscious changes as required by the frog must be undergone volitionally. We *will* them. Therefore, the Princess, though she is nauseated by the whole process, fulfills the conditions of her promise by gritting her teeth and doing it.

Much Christian growth comes through an act of the will. When we forgive our enemies seventy times seven, when we pray for them and do good to them who have despitefully used us, it is will power in action. When Jesus asked the rich young man to sell all he had, give it to the poor and follow him, this was an appeal to his will. Loving is not always liking but rather being kind or fair to one who is the most unlovable, such as a slimy frog. Yet God honors what we do because it is right or appropriate, regardless of how we feel about it. Then, as it were, the frog turns into a Prince and the Princess enters into a new life because she has been faithful to the Word.

So often we miss the working of God in our lives because the task, the person, the attitude we are being asked to accept is such an earthy, frog-like thing. Learning a new language, acquiring a new skill, acknowledging your sexuality, taking time for quiet and meditation, treating your body with respect, eating the correct food, treating a parent, child or neighbor with patience may be a small price to pay for inner wholeness. If we could make an image of what is being asked of us, it might appear as a disgusting frog. But if God is behind the demand, in retrospect it will become to us not a frog but a handsome Prince. A transformation has occurred. Something in us has been born in a strange, mysterious way.

It is always worth asking what you have promised yourself or another—something you tend to minimize or discount to everyone's hurt.

Two years ago a dentist friend of mine with a flourishing practice promised himself that he would take more time away from the office each week. For the ensuing months he continually procrastinated on this promise. He told himself it wasn't *that* important. He was too busy. He didn't know what he would do with all that free time. But in so doing he paid a price. He became more and more harried, lost his temper at home and at the office, had no peace of mind. Meanwhile, his inner frog continually knocked at his door. Recently, he consented to the frog's demand and is now taking every Friday off.

Who knows? Even Jesus may appear to you as an unwanted frog tapping persistently upon your door.

The Spirit in the Bottle

Once upon a time there was a poor woodcutter. He had an only son, whom he wished to send to a university. However, since he could give his son only a little money to take with him to college, it was used up long before the time for examinations. So the son went home and helped his father with the work in the forest.

Once, during the Friday rest, he roamed the woods and came to an immense old oak, where he heard a voice calling from the ground, "Let me out, let me out." He dug down among the roots of the tree and found a well-sealed bottle from which the voice had clearly come. He opened it. Instantly a spirit rushed out and quickly became half as high as the tree.

This spirit spoke to him and said, "I have had my punishment, and now I will be revenged. I am the great and mighty Mercury, and you have set me free; therefore I must break your neck." This made the young man uneasy. Quickly thinking up a trick, he said, "But first I must be sure that you are the same little spirit which was shut up in the bottle." As proof, the spirit crept back into the bottle. Then the young man made haste to seal the spirit in the bottle and captured it in this way. But now the spirit promised to reward him if he would let it out. So he let it out and received as a reward a small piece of cloth. When he wiped his broken axe with this rag, the axe turned to silver and he was able to sell it for four hundred thaler.

Thus father and son were freed from all their worries. And the young man could return to his studies. Later, thanks to the rag, he became a famous doctor.

■ ■ ■

When I was a boy, Halloween was more a night for "tricks" than for "treats." When the gang got out on the street, the mercurial spirit popped out of the bottle. We felt we had implied permission to be devilish. We threw paint bombs, pulled streetcars off their cables, hoisted garbage cans onto telephone poles. Nice kids turned into a bunch of hoodlums with no concern for anybody's property.

Actually, the mercurial spirit can be released any time the social, ethical, religious or political constraints that have kept it sealed and bottled up are removed. When it bursts forth, it may grow to such proportions that it threatens to overpower us. The French or Communist revolutions, the race and anti-Vietnam riots of the sixties, the sexual permissiveness of our day are instances of such a spirit breaking loose. The problem, of course, is that there is often something positive in the mercurial spirit; some change is necessary, but a creative, not destructive one.

Thinking symbolically, this sort of difficulty faced the woodcutter's son when he uncorked the bottle beneath the tree. A new spirit was necessary to transform his situation. However, what came forth might have destroyed him.

Notice it is a "mercurial" spirit because it is so hard to handle and can be splintered into little pieces that go one way or another.

When St. Paul emphasized to Jew and Greek in Corinth that they were saved not by obeying the Torah (Law) or by doing good works but by faith in Jesus Christ, he also loosed the mercurial spirit in the community. Christian liberty became Christian license. Paul was shocked and wrote:

> "All things are lawful for me," but not all things are helpful. (1 Cor. 6:12)
> Do not be deceived; neither the immoral, nor idolators, nor adulterers, nor sexual perverts, nor thieves, nor the greedy, nor drunkards, nor revilers, nor robbers will inherit the kingdom of God. (1 Cor. 6:9, 10)

Like the woodcutter's son, Paul was faced with the task of getting the spirit back into the bottle and then letting it out again in a constructive manner.

40

The normal reaction to the mercurial spirit is to use force to get it under control. When Moses left the Israelites in the wilderness to be alone with God on Mt. Sinai, the people felt deserted and turned to other gods. They feasted before the golden calf, ate, drank and rose up to play. All their pent-up energies, over which Moses had tightly reigned, came forth in a wild fertility rite. Moses' response on his return was swift and terrible:

> ". . . then Moses stood in the gate of the camp, and said, "Who is on the Lord's side? Come to me." And all the sons of Levi gathered themselves together to him. And he said to them, "Thus says the Lord God of Israel. Put every man his sword on his side, and go to and fro from gate to gate throughout the camp, and slay every man his brother, and every man his companions, and every man his neighbor." (Exodus 32:26-27)

Such drastic action is reminiscent of Russian armies invading Hungary and Czechoslovakia, stuffing the mercurial spirit in those countries back into a particular Communist bottle and burying it underground. Any positive aspect of this burst of creative energy is altogether lost. Likewise with the people of Israel: they were doomed to wander forty years before they were prepared to possess the promised land. Moses did not enter it at all.

What is needed is some way of getting the mercurial spirit contained and then releasing it to be a blessing rather than a curse so that it may bring forth symbolically the piece of cloth which turned the woodcutter's axe to silver.

In the Jewish tradition, the Torah (Law) was designed to unlock the creative spirit within certain limits or boundaries. But over the years, it, too, encased the Spirit of God behind laws become archaic, the interpretation of these laws and the interpretation of the interpretations. As Jesus said, new wine needed to be put into new wineskins. It came as the Holy Spirit fell upon the disciples on the Feast of Pentecost.

Over the centuries, however, the same difficulty arises within the Christian community again and again. The question is always how the Christian Church deals with the mercurial spirit, be it in a social revolution involving sexual mores, a political struggle to liberate the poor and exploited, or in a new pentecostal movement offering religious experience. Each of these can release a mercurial spirit holding the seeds of destruction and devisiveness on the one hand or creative renewal on the other.

In our tale, the woodcutter's son entices the spirit back into the bottle by asking, "Are you really the same spirit that was in that little bottle?" There is no coercion in such a stratagem. And, as Hanna Arendt has pointed out, the moment you resort to violence, you have already lost your power over another and are likely to cause more harm than good.

By the same token, the only way to get a mercurial spirit back into a Christian bottle is to challenge whether it truly reflects the love, the mind and the purpose of Christ. The Christian container is the Church united to its crucified and risen Lord and committed to the spread of Christ's Kingdom in the world. If you are filled with the mercurial spirit and claim to be a Christian, you can be asked to test your faith by climbing back into the bottle. Are you still the same spirit that was there when the Church began?

In each age, mercurial spirits must come out of the bottle if there is to be new and creative life; but to be Holy Spirit, they need to be channeled by the love of Christ. This is especially true within the Church itself.

When the mercurial spirit in our story is re-corked and comes forth a second time, it brings with it the cloth that turns the axe to silver. This is the same kind of blessing our Lord promises his disciples who remain close to him.

I am the true vine, and my Father is the vinedresser . . . . Abide in me, and I in you. As the branch cannot bear fruit by itself, unless it abides in the vine, neither can you, unless you abide in me. I am the vine, you are the branches. He who abides in me, and I in him, he it is that bears much fruit . . . . (John 15:1, 4-5)

Hansel and Gretel

Long ago a poor woodcutter lived at the edge of a large forest with his two children, Hansel and Gretel, and their stepmother. It happened that there was a famine in the land, and the woodcutter's family scarcely had enough to eat. As a result, the stepmother suggested to the woodcutter that they take their children into the woods and leave them there, since this would be better than watching them starve to death.

However, the children overheard their parents talking. When they entered the woods Hansel left a trail of stones behind them, and they were able to find their way home again. Nevertheless, the famine continued. Again, the stepmother urged her husband to lose his children in the woods. This time Hansel dropped bread-crumbs to mark the way home, but birds ate them. The boy and his sister found themselves alone and lost in the great forest.

By the next day Hansel and Gretel were very hungry. They followed a snow-white bird that was singing sweetly and were led to a cottage made of ginger-bread, its roof of cakes and window-panes of candy.

Unfortunately for the children, the house was owned by a wicked witch who liked to eat little boys and girls. The witch put Hansel in a cage and forced Gretel to do her housework. Indeed, she would have devoured both of them if Gretel had not tricked her and pushed the witch into the oven, slamming the door shut.

In the witch's cottage they discovered some precious pearls and stones. And with the help of a white duck who carried them across a lake, they were able to return home. When the children arrived, they discovered their step-mother had died. Their father rejoiced to see them. Thanks to the jewels, the woodcutter's family never wanted for anything again.

■ ■ ■

Students of Swiss psychoanalyst Carl Gustav Jung have suggested that fairy tales may accurately describe the unconscious psychic difficulties of a given culture or particular age, while at the same time offering symbolic solution to the same problems. In this sense, the story itself may be a gift of God.

Viewed in this light, our tale depicts a period of spiritual poverty, i.e., when famine overruns the land. In Jung's categories, the masculine / feminine principles in man, represented by the father and stepmother, are respectively weak and negative; therefore, the children are in danger of death. In ancient legends, when the King was ill, the land suffered. So here the ineffectiveness of the father and the selfishness of the stepmother portray a collective condition in which the "feminine" and "masculine" elements in the social fabric have soured and gone bad.

According to Jung, the feminine principle is that capacity in every male or female that facilitates harmonious relationships and seeks to reconcile differences. It includes a loving concern for people, their nurture and growth, a sensitivity for values.

The masculine principle, on the other hand, is man's ability to separate out and identify differences, causal connections and goals. It is the capacity to differentiate, to clarify issues. The masculine principle divides in order to understand and to achieve ends. The feminine unites in order that love and peace may prevail. Men and women alike have both principles within them to a greater or lesser degree, although the masculine tends to predominate in men and the feminine in women. Both elements need to be realized positively if a person is to be whole individually or a society healthy corporately.

In our fairy tale, the feminine symbol of the stepmother is obviously destructive since she is willing to cast the children to the wolves. Moreover, the father is equally inadequate for he is unwilling to protect his two offspring and unable to discover solutions for their problems.

It is thus an interesting exercise to speculate on the areas in our western culture in which both the masculine and feminine capacities have failed to the detriment of children, literally or figuratively, as new creative possibilities open to the human race. For Christians, it would certainly be the failure of man's resolve, insight and compassion to eliminate war, hunger and human exploitation. A Hitler may be vanquished, but nations still look at one another with mutual suspicion and fear. Every advance in science is an opportunity for a few, who possess the knowledge, to withhold it from others or share it only for a price. It is the Hansels and Gretels, the young, the new, who are left in the wilderness to die of machine gun bullets, malnutrition and harsh child labor. Until society is filled with the love of Christ who prayed for his enemies and taught us to hammer expectantly at God for the answers to our problems, these human dilemmas are unlikely to change.

In our tale, Hansel and Gretel, of course, go from the frying pan into the fire. They become controlled by the devouring witch who seduces them with her cottage made of candy, cakes and other goodies, imprisons Hansel in a cage and plans to consume them both.

What better picture of a consumer-oriented society in which the main effort is to provide for the pleasure, comfort and protection of all. It is as though the masculine principle (represented by the father), with its harsher demands to meet some calculated ends, has abdicated its responsibility. The only answer is to produce more and more goods and services to gratify more and more needs. The result so often is narcissistic, soft young people unable to mature or an adult population unwilling to take any resolute steps to deal, for example, with an energy crisis. Hansel is encaged. Gretel is confined to the home. The feminine witch fattens them up for her own satisfaction. Again, the fairy tale has in

45

its own symbolic way described the next step of our western psychic process where we reject new possibilities by consuming them before they can unfold. Our frantic desire for food, pleasure, comfort and entertainment makes any new evolution impossible. However, there is hope. Gretel, the new feminine possibility, rebels and pushes the devouring witch into the oven, the locus of transformation where anything is made assimilable. Here may be our women's liberation movement at its best, challenging the current value structure in our society: the double standard ethic, the destructive side of women in the home, the unwillingness of a male-dominated culture to tackle crying social problems in new creative ways. By her action Gretel releases her brother and brings hope to her father; for when the children return home, they bring the jewels with them from the witch's house. Significantly, the stepmother has now died. The negative feminine has been overcome. Yet even more importantly, a mature feminine figure has not yet taken her place. It is the fairy tale's way of saying that salvation in the situation has begun but has not yet been accomplished. Only a mature positive feminine figure, united with a revived masculine power, can finally make society what Divine Providence desires it to be.

All these reflections may seem far removed from the fact that the Kingdom of God is breaking into our midst; and yet, if the fairy tale is symbolically indicating what is happening, (in part unconsciously) in the psyche of our culture, God is at work doing a new thing. How often in the New Testament the Kingdom is prefigured as the uniting of masculine and feminine as in a marriage or wedding feast. Even the Book of Revelation pictures the culmination of the Kingdom as the New Jerusalem coming down out of heaven like a bride adorned for her husband. It is another way of affirming that the realization of human completeness and fulfillment is the joining of understanding with love, knowledge with compassion, insight with will, masculine with feminine. God's providence may thus be discerned through a fairy tale if we have the eyes to see and ears with which to understand.

The Cobbler and the Tailor

Hill and valley never meet, but God's children do. And so it happened that a Cobbler and Tailor met on the road and agreed to travel together. The Tailor was a happy, easy-going man who shared his bread and earnings with the Cobbler. The Cobbler, on the other hand, was surly and bad-tempered—so much so that people did not like to deal with him at all.

After a time, the two men came to a great forest. Here they discovered two paths leading to the next city—one taking seven days, the other, two. Neither man knew which path was the shortest. The Cobbler insisted on carrying a seven day's worth of load on his back, but the Tailor didn't wish to carry such a burden and trusted that God would provide for him. Unfortunately for the Tailor, the men chose the longer way. By the morning of the fifth day the Tailor was so hungry he begged the Cobbler for some food. After all, he pointed out, he had shared with the Cobbler freely in days past. "I will give you a scrap," replied the Cobbler, "but it will cost you one eye." The Tailor had no choice, so the Cobbler cut out an eye with a sharp knife. Two days later the Tailor was so famished he again pleaded for help. The Cobbler agreed, but cut out his other eye and left the blind Tailor under a gallows in the forest.

Now it happened that there were two dead men hanging there, and upon the head of each was a crow. One of the dead men spoke to the other, saying that if a blind man would but wipe his eyes with the dew that dripped from the gallows, his sight would return. When the Tailor heard this, he took his handkerchief, pressed it to the grass and wiped the moist dew over the sockets of his eyes. Immediately his sight returned.

Thanking God for his recovery, the Tailor began his journey once again. Along the path he came across a foal, a stork, some ducks and some bees making honey. All of them begged him not to hurt them, and although the Tailor was desperately hungry, he did not touch them yet managed to reach the city. Within a short time, because of his skill and manner, the Tailor was attached to the court of the King. The Cobbler also had risen to Court Cobbler and naturally feared that the Tailor would seek revenge. He therefore privately told the King that the Tailor could do one great deed and then another. The Tailor would never have met these tests but for the help given him by the foal, the stork, the duck and the bees which he had befriended.

In the end the Cobbler was forced to leave the city. His way took him by the gallows. While he was asleep, the two crows sitting on the hanged men's heads pecked out his eyes. He was never seen again. "My mother was right," says the Tailor, "If a man trusts God and if he's lucky, he cannot fail."

■ ■ ■

The Bible describes contrasting people, like our tailor and cobbler, who come into conflict because they hold opposing attitudes and points of view. Cain and Abel, Jacob and Esau, Mary and Martha, the Prodigal and Elder Sons come to mind. The question is always whether the two can reconcile their differences or whether their struggle with one another will end in total alienation or disaster.

It is interesting to note that such pairs of opposites as the tailor and cobbler have both positive and negative aspects to their personalities. The tailor, for example, is an extrovert who lives in the present. He is generous to a fault because he trusts in God. The Cobbler, on the other hand, dislikes people and must look out for himself since he does not believe any providential hand will provide for him.

While the tailor is the more attractive of the two, his happy-go-lucky attitude results in his being unmindful of the consequences of his unnecessary risks. The fact is that the two need one another, and each might have learned from the other's strengths if either had been willing to do so.

The Holy Scriptures begin, as it were, with the same kind of conflict in the persons of Cain and Abel. Canon Wedel has called the Cain and Abel incident the first murder in the cathedral. While the two brothers were worshipping God in the offering of sacrifice, the killing occurred. The Bible tells us little about the two men except that Cain was a farmer and Abel a shepherd. However, the Letter to the Hebrews suggests that Abel's offering was acceptable to God because he had *faith*, whereas Cain did not. If faith in this context means, as J.B. Phillips defines it, "the faculty for perceiving invisible realities," then Cain, probably an earthy, sense-oriented man, may have deeply resented his brother's intuitive awareness of God. Instead of accepting their differences and his own unique gifts, Cain kills Abel out of anger and jealousy, only to discover that, while he may eliminate his brother, he cannot slay his conscience or his God.

The differences between Jacob and Esau are clearer. Esau is pictured as a strong, hairy outdoorsman whose main concerns are hunting for game and filling his stomach. Jacob is more inward and clever, with an eye to the future like the cobbler. Esau, tailor-like, is willing to trade his birthright for a good meal. Jacob has no compunction about tricking his blind father, Isaac, into giving him his blessing instead of his brother. Esau is not conscious enough to prevent it.

Whereas the Cain and Abel tale ends in tragedy, the reconciliation between Jacob and Esau is one of the most touching scenes in all of Scripture. Jacob wisely fled Esau's wrath, escaping to Mesopotamia. When he returns home years later with wives, family and cattle, Esau comes out to meet him with a large force. After wrestling with God all night, Jacob courageously faces his brother. When Esau embraces him, Jacob exclaims, "Truly to see your face is like seeing the face of God." Unlike the cobbler, Jacob has

49

confronted the man he has hurt so badly. The history of Israel became the story of the people of God because Jacob was willing to take that risk and Esau was willing to be the instrument of God's forgiveness.

Christians can well heed our Lord's own words in this regard: ". . . if you are offering your gift at the altar, and there remember that your brother has something against you, leave your gift there before the altar and go; first be reconciled to your brother, and then come and offer your gift" (Mt. 5:23, 24).

C.G. Jung believed each of us has a shadow—an undeveloped side to ourselves—symbolized in dreams and stories by the persons of the same age and sex, such as the tailor and the cobbler or Cain and Abel. Jack Sanford has characterized these inferior parts of our personality as the inner adversary—the person within us whose thoughts and feelings contradict our outer front. He / she is the one we try to hide—usually unsuccessfully—a kind of Mr. Hyde to Dr. Jekyll. Religious people are likely to deny their shadows, which means they project their darkness upon others while outwardly presenting a facade of moral or pious sanctity. Jung in his autobiography tells of his visit to a certain holy man. For several days, he writes, he became more and more depressed by his own religious limitations until he met the wife of the devout man. All the holy man's unlived and denied life had been dumped upon her. This fact relieved Jung immensely but did little for the wife. For when our shadow sides go unrecognized, they come out in destructive ways upon those that are closest to us.

In his book, *The Kingdom Within*, Jack Sanford explores the dynamic of the unconscious shadow in our Lord's words:

> Come to terms with your opponent in good time while you are still on the way to the court with him, or he may hand you over to the judge and the judge to the officer and you will be thrown into prison. I tell you solemnly, you will not get out till you have paid the last penny. (Mt. 5:25-26).

As he points out, if Jesus had in mind a literal lawsuit

with an outer opponent, there is no reason why we should always be the ones to be held guilty. However, if it is our inner adversary with whom we must come to terms, then the case is different. As Jack Sanford put it:

> For it is the task of consciousness to recognize, face, and be reconciled with every aspect of our total self. If we fail to do so, we have to reckon with the larger authority within us—that is, with the court of the King—and we then must pay a bitter price by experiencing in a negative way what we have denied.[6]

Mary and Martha are a case in point. Most women will admit they have both qualities within them—a desire for deep personal relationship such as Mary exhibited for Jesus; and a conscientious, responsible, organized side that is determined to treat guests properly as in the case of Martha. As sisters so often are, Mary and Martha are shadow aspects of one another.

However, it is the parable of the prodigal son and elder brother that brings out our shadow sides in the finest detail. The first has wasted his inheritance with riotous living; the second has stayed home working the fields for his father. Why should the father welcome his young son back with such joy, kill the fatted calf, put a ring on his finger, shoes on his feet and call in the neighbors to celebrate the prodigal son's return? Despite the father's remonstrances, the elder son refuses to join the festivities—and understandably so.

If you see here a picture of two sides of your own personality, the parable describes a moment when forgiveness is being offered but a part of you refuses to accept it. The elder son in you demands further guilt and punishment. You are being kept out of the Kingdom because two sides of you cannot be reconciled.

Outwardly the impasse between the prodigal son and elder brother is of a moral man who cannot forgive his own immoral brother.

Still, the prodigal and elder bothers need one another.

51

If the prodigal will not face the collective wisdom epitomized by his older brother, he will never grow to be the person God is calling him to be. If the older brother will not deal with his own failure to love, he will never experience the glow of the Kingdom of God.

Thus from a Christian perspective the fate of the cobbler in our fairy tale is not a triumph of goodness over evil but the common human tragedy of failing to seek God's grace to transform evil into good. Only reconciliation can bring this change about. Unlike Jacob, the cobbler does not change his attitudes, seek forgiveness and new life. Unlike Esau, the tailor does not have the opportunity to forgive the deep wounds inflicted upon him.

Unfortunately, many Christians watching their television sets see the good guys triumphing over the bad guys — evil getting its just desserts — as the desirable outcome. It isn't. Cain wandering unforgiven, the elder son pouting outside the home, Mary and Martha estranged from one another are Christian *failures*.

Who knows? If Judas Iscariot had sought forgiveness instead of suicide he might have become the greatest disciple of them all.

PART II
THE TRILOGY
OF THE RING

The Lord of the Rings

Tolkien's trilogy, *The Lord of the Rings*, is the story of the great war of the Ring which occurred in the third age of Middle-earth. This land is inhabited by creatures like ourselves as well as others strange and different, for in this world are wizards, dwarves, elves, orcs, goblins, ring-wraiths, tree-ents as well as friendly furry-footed people called hobbits. The natural environment is also alive with purposeful activity boding both good and evil for anyone who ventures into it.

The hero of the tale is a hobbit, named Frodo, whose Uncle Bilbo had accidentally come into possession of the Master Ring of great power some years before.

The story begins when Gandalf the Grey, a wizard of no mean repute, discovers that Bilbo, the hobbit, has the Ring in his possession. Moreover, the wizard's travels make him aware that already Sauron, the Evil One, who had this Ring forged for himself, likewise suspected that it might be in the Shire populated by the hobbits. Already the black riders of Mordor are stealthily moving around the Shire, bent on finding and returning the Ring to their Overlord.

Now this One Ring of power had been forged genera-tions earlier by dwarves of another age. Each time it is used it turns the bearer invisible. Each time the bearer exercises its power he becomes more possessed by the Ring itself. Ultimately, it will corrupt anyone, even those who use the Ring with highest motives.

In a previous battle against the Evil One, the Ring had

been cut from Sauron's finger before its power had been maximized. It was later found and protected by a strange, slimy creature named Gollum, from whose clutches Bilbo took it. Gollum called the Ring "his precious" and turns up in the story attempting to regain it.

Getting back to the tale, Gandalf, the wizard, acquaints Bilbo with the danger. But because Bilbo is getting old, Gandalf encourages his nephew, Frodo, to bear the Ring as far as Rivendell where they can get the advice of Elrond, the ancient patriarch of the elves. Frodo sets out with the Ring in his pocket, accompanied by his servant, Samwise, and his kinsmen, Meriadoc and Peregrin. Gandalf, too, has agreed to assist them along the way.

The journey to Rivendell makes them all conscious of the tremendous danger they are in. The black riders upon horses with a keen sense of smell follow them along the way. The natural environment of swamps and barrow-downs cast their own spells. Everywhere evil lurks as well as friendly forces that offer to support them. Badly shaken, they are fortunate to arrive at Rivendell in one piece

At Rivendell, Elrond calls a Council to decide what must be done to defend themselves against Sauron's rising might and how to handle the Ring so Sauron cannot regain it. The strategy adopted was to warn those people not yet under Sauron's spell and ready them for battle. In the meantime the Ring of Power must be totally destroyed by casting it into the volcanic fire from which it was forged, located on Mt. Doom in the heart of the enemy's territory—Mordor itself. Frodo offers to bear the Ring. With him are chosen eight companions: Gandalf the Wizard; three other hobbits; Legolas, son of the elven King; Gimli, the dwarf; along with Aragorn and Boromir, representing the race of men.

The stage is now set for all that will follow. The enemy, Sauron—the Evil One—lacks only the One Ring to cement his power. With him are armies of orcs and goblins, not to mention the men and dwarves that already have been entrapped by his deadly influence.

United in resistance are the free peoples of Middle-earth—the men of Rohan and Gondar, the elves of Rivendell and powerful tree-ents who are roused to battle.

When Frodo and his eight companions are frustrated in their attempt to cross the high pass of Caradhras in winter, Gandalf leads them through a hidden gate into the Mines of Moria beneath the mountain. There Gandalf falls into a dark abyss in a battle with a Nazgul — a dreadful spirit of the underworld.

Aragorn is now revealed as the hidden heir of the ancient Kings of the West. He leads the company through the elvish land of Lorien to the Falls of Rauros where a decision is called for — whether to go with Boromir to the aid of Minas Tirith, the chief city of Gondor, or to continue towards Mt. Doom. At this point Boromir attempts to seize the Ring but fails. The company is then divided. Frodo continues with his servant Samwise towards Mt. Doom. Boromir repents and dies gallantly. The hobbits, Meriadoc and Peregrin, are captured but later rescued by Aragorn. The Riders of Rohan and ents led by Treebeard go into battle. The fate of Minas Tirith hangs in the balance.

Meanwhile, Frodo and Samwise, pursued by Gollum, who at one time had the ring, struggle to find their way to Mt. Doom. At the final moment, with success within reach, the Ring so possesses Frodo that he cannot throw it into the fiery cauldron. However, Gollum bites it off his finger and then topples into the volcano, sealing Sauron's fate. Thus ends the Third Age of Middle-earth. The Dominion of Man begins.

Frodo is so transformed by all that has befallen him that he can no longer live comfortably in the Shire. It is his destiny now to follow the elves and dwarves sailing to the great Havens of the West.

■ ■ ■

The Quest or Inner Journey

The Road goes ever on and on
Down from the door where it began.
Now far ahead the Road has gone,
And I must follow, if I can.
Pursuing it with weary feet,
Until it joins some larger way,
Where many paths and errands meet.
And whither then? I cannot say.[1]

Anyone visiting Canterbury Cathedral can see indentations in the stone floors and steps that have been literally worn down over the centuries by pilgrims who have traveled great distances to worship there.

And whether it be Canterbury, Rome, Jerusalem, Mecca or Benares, the journey to the holy place to find God or be found by him is as natural for you and for me as our thirst for water. In fact, our lives can be pictured as a pilgrimage shaped by outer events, but just as much as a journey into the depths within ourselves as towards places without.

Therefore, it is no accident that such Christian literature as Dante's *Divine Comedy*, the *Legend of the Holy Grail* or Bunyan's *Pilgrim's Progress* describes a Christian's growth under the symbol of a quest—a search for holiness or wholeness. Indeed, when our Lord admonishes us to be perfect as your heavenly Father is perfect (Mt. 5:48), he is not expecting sinlessness, absolute goodness or an absence of mistakes. Rather he is reminding you and me that we have a God-given drive towards completeness, towards fulfillment which we realize dynamically as we love others as God loves us — sending his sun and rain equally upon the evil as well as the good. This process is not ideal. It involves reconciliation, confrontations, wrestling for consciousness and the daily openness to God.

If you look at *The Lord of the Rings* as expressing this quest for wholeness common to us all, you will note that nothing is repeated. Frodo goes from one encounter to the next. And while there are interludes of rest and refreshment, such as at Rivendell and Lorien, the need to complete the quest is ever before him.

You and I may experience this drive towards wholeness as a curious restlessness, a craving for adventure, a dissatisfaction with ourselves, or, as in the Ring story, the sense that evil is threatening to engulf us. Nothing like having the dark riders of Mordor chasing you to alert you that something needs to be changed. But whatever the age or circumstance, the drive is the same — to become who we are by leaving the security of familiar things and risking the unknown, either outwardly or inwardly — usually a combination of both.

W.H. Auden has offered the following typology of quest literature that may explain our interest in mythology, mystery stories and tales of buried treasure:
1. A precious object or person is to be found, possessed, married, etc.
2. A long journey or effort is needed to find it, the whereabouts originally not known by the seekers.
3. A hero must uncover the object since what is to be found or accomplished cannot be by anybody but only by those who possess the right qualities or character.
4. A test or series of tests must be passed by which the unworthy are screened out and the hero revealed.
5. The guardians of the object must be overcome before the quest is won.
6. Helpers who have knowledge and power assist the hero and but for them the hero would never succeed.

Clearly *The Lord of the Rings* fits this pattern. Only in this case the objective is to dispose of and destroy the Ring rather than find and possess it. Moreover, Frodo has the right attributes for the task. He is tenacious but humble

—thereby less likely to fall under the Ring's spell. Jesus tells us that the pure in heart shall see God and that the meek shall inherit the earth. If the pure in heart have singleness of purpose and the meek are those who accept what life offers and what life demands, then Frodo possesses these qualities. Moreover, he had eight companions, as our Lord had his disciples, which is indicative that you and I will not complete our quest without the aid of friends.

In his book, *The Hero with a Thousand Faces*, Joseph Campbell notes, like Auden, how legends, fairy tales and religious epics the world over depict heroes and heroines who have been called to this courageous spiritual journey. Often they are given talismans to protect them against danger, as Frodo was offered a sword and coat of mail. But there comes a time, according to Campbell, when the hero reaches a moment of decision where success lies in his own hands. It is like Frodo at Tol Brandir and our Lord in the wilderness. If this final test is successfully passed, the hero will return home where everything is the same yet all is different. For the pilgrim now brings to his / her life the magic of compassion—a desire to live out life for love rather than for mere survival or personal gain.

In the everydayness of your life and mine, it is not always obvious that you and I are living out our own quests —that we are the potential heroes and heroines of our own epic tales. We may even be unaware that God is calling us as our Lord did his disciples, or as Gandalf beckoned Frodo out of the sheltered environment in which he was living. Actually, God's call and our response may be so gradual that we may have left port without realizing we are out to sea. But when we begin, you and I must pass into that dimension of Reality Jesus called the Kingdom of God—go into a new depth within our very selves even as we are facing problems in the outside world. And since Christians must not take lightly the polarity of having one foot on this earth and another in the Kingdom, here are some insights from *The Lord of the Rings* and the New Testament that may guide you on your way.

1. The initial pull of the Kingdom is to develop your own ego-strength so that you are capable of coping with

the outside world. In other words, it is unwise to prematurely push for the inner journey into the Kingdom of God. Frodo was in his late fifties before he was ready to leave the Shire. Living with his uncle Bilbo and handling Bilbo's property gave him the self-assurance necessary later on. Our Lord became a skilled carpenter, grew in wisdom before God and man before his baptism by John the Baptist in the river Jordan. It was only then that the Holy Spirit fell upon him like a dove. The essential first is a degree of genuine confidence in our own abilities and self-worth. I recall a learned criminologist recounting that as a young farm boy of five, a sickly neighbor paid him a nickel to lead his cattle in and out of pasture. If the boy did not do his job, the cattle were not fed. As a result, at this early age the lad was acquiring a sense of responsibility and a certain capability about dealing with real problems that the modern boy does not get by emptying the garbage.

By the same token, Indian tribes had tests for adolescent boys, like killing their first buffalo, that gave assurance that they were ready to be "Brave."

Nor must we forget that our Lord sent his disciples out two by two to heal the sick, cleanse the lepers and preach the Kingdom—do the very things that they had watched him do long before he left them to journey by themselves.

The first stage of the spiritual journey paradoxically demands that you and I develop confidence in ourselves in handling people or things mainly in the outer world.

2. When you are called out of the familiar shire—into the Kingdom so to speak—you are in the realm where Jesus Christ not only is Lord but also is available to you. In the Trilogy, Gandalf the Grey performs the same role. It is he who starts Frodo on his quest and goes ahead of him to prepare the way—turning up at critical moments to reverse the tide.

Thus the second important step for Christians in our personal journey is to develop a personal relationship with the risen Lord. The companionship we have with Jesus is the greatest resource Christians have which non-Christians may not consciously know. For not only does Jesus make us aware of the Kingdom and call us into it, but we encounter him as we enter it. To discover for ourselves that Jesus has been resurrected from the dead is to find ourselves in the Kingdom of God. To live in the Kingdom is to enter a realm where Jesus is at work and alive.

The late William Temple has suggested that our Lord's familiar words in John's Gospel can be paraphrased:

> Let not your hearts be troubled; believe in God; believe also in me. In my Father's house are many way stations (not mansions or rooms). If it were not so I would have told you. And when I go, I will prepare a place for you and I will come again and take you to myself that where I am there you may be also.[8]

In this sense, like Gandalf, our Lord is an advance guard going on ahead of us and yet continually returning to be with us until the end of the age.

3. Even after you become aware of the Kingdom of God, there will be a tendency to give up the quest out of lassitude, laziness or despair. When Frodo and his hobbit companions started out, the first obstacle they met was the Old Forest where they were overcome with drowsiness. The trees threatened to envelop them; in fact, Pippin and Merry were trapped in the trunk of one of them.

It is amazing how our first burning desires to journey on the spiritual quest can so quickly disappear at the onslaught of old fears, habit patterns that lead us straight back to unconsciousness. If you have ever attempted to follow a diet or rule of life, you have a good idea of the inertia that can hobble you from walking in the Kingdom. Hence, Jesus tells the parable of the Sower whose seeds fall on rocky ground where the birds of the air eat them or where they take no root. It is easy to backslide in the Kingdom when we are caught up in the pressures of the everyday world or to lose heart when adversity comes.

But perhaps the greatest discouragement is the wave of despair or hopelessness that at times is overpowering. In *The Lord of the Rings*, a huge winged being—a Nazgul—hovers over the forces of Theoden in the field Pelennor, causing panic and fear, threatening to turn the tide for Sauron.

. . . suddenly in the midst of the glory of the king his golden shield was dimmed. The new morning was blotted from the sky. Dark fell about him. Horses reared and screamed. Men cast from the saddle lay grovelling on the ground . . . .

The great shadow descended like a falling cloud. And behold! it was a winged creature . . . .

Upon it sat a shape, black-mantled, huge and threatening. A crown of steel he bore, but between rim and robe naught was there to see, save the deadly gleam of eyes: the Lord of the Nazgul.[9]

Each year the Christian community recites the events of the Passion in which the disciples are scattered, Jesus imprisoned, tried and crucified—when darkness covered all the land. It was the black moment of despair when all seemed worthless or hopeless.

In the same way St. John of the Cross speaks of the "dark night of the soul" when all efforts to continue your spiritual adventure turn to ashes, when events turn against you—when you run dry. And it is the glory both of the Gospel and the Ring story that these aspects of the quest are not denied. For unless you know they are coming, the quest will begin in a Pollyannaish fashion and end with the first threat of failure or onslaught of boredom.

4. Companions on your journey are essential. Without the support of the eight that went with him, Frodo would never have reached Mt. Doom, and without his disciples our Lord's work here on earth would never have been carried on.

The greatest sacrament of them all, the one that is almost always discounted or forgotten—the fellowship of the Christian community. Within that Body and sometimes from without, you will need to find selected persons who will journey with you for a time, bearing your burdens, praying for you, even as you at moments support them. The key people may change, just as first Peter, then Paul or others affected the lives of the early Christians; as first Virgil, a pagan, then Beatrice led Dante towards paradise .

In the past the Church raised up "spiritual directors" —

men or women who understood the problems of living and growing in the Kingdom. So today small groups and wise directors are necessary if we are to share with one another our varying gifts and be comrades on the way.

5. Evil is real. It is within you as well as outside of you. When our Lord goes through his initial temptations Satan departs from him "for a time." It is always there. In the Trilogy, Sauron, the Evil One, ebbs and flows with power, is thwarted but never fully vanquished. Yet evil is no match for conscious sacrificial love. Sauron, for example, cannot imagine that anyone would give up the Ring or attempt to destroy it. However, unless evil is brought out into the open, confronted and battled, it will take possession of the best of us.

In the New Testament you see Satan being cast out of heaven, becoming consciously visible on earth through the light cast by the ministry of Jesus Christ and those in whom he lives. For example, the demonic aspects of Church and State are exposed in the actions of Caiaphas, the high priest, and Pontius Pilate, the governor, who use the well-being of these institutions to cloak their own fears and acceptance of injustice. It is not the collective organizations that are bad, but they can exercise a destructive as well as beneficial influence, especially when dominated by selfish, blind or weak-hearted men through whom evil may work. Moreover, nothing is more demonic than a potentially good and great person fallen prey to the Evil One, as was the case of Saruman, the wizard in the story of the Ring. Holed up in his tower at Orthanc, Saruman could use words so smoothly that he could sway others with his spell. Of him Tolkien writes:

> Suddenly another voice spoke, low and melodious, its very sound an enchantment. Those who listened unwarily to that voice could seldom report the words that they heard . . . Mostly they remembered only that it was a delight to hear the voice speaking, all that it said seemed wise and reasonable, and desire awoke in them by swift agreement to seem wise themselves . . . .

It was Gimli the dwarf who broke in suddenly, 'The words of this wizard stand on their heads . . . . In the language of Orthanc help means ruin, and saving means slaying, that is plain.'[10]

To face Saruman was to encounter the devil in a wizard. In the tale of the Ring it took a Gandalf—another wizard—who had gone through the gauntlet of sacrifice to drive such evil into light, just as in the Gospels Jesus Christ could cast out demons and liberate persons from their spell.

So it is that the deeper or farther one moves on one's spiritual journey, the more one is aware of the demonic that lies inside and outside ourselves often hidden behind a facade of "good."

Such comments may make the journey appear an awesome task. In one sense it is, but to take it consciously with your eyes open is by far the safest course. Most importantly, it is a pilgrimage which God calls each of us to take. Because it is of God, it is a journey which, with grace, we can truly make.

The Use of Power

Three Rings for the Elven-kings under the sky,
   Seven for the Dwarf-lords in their halls of stone,
Nine for the Mortal Men doomed to die,
   One for the Dark Lord on his dark throne.
In the land of Mordor where the Shadows lie
   One Ring to rule them all, One Ring to find them,
One Ring to bring them all and in the darkness bind
      them
   In the land of Mordor where the Shadows lie.[11]

Thus does the ballad extol the power of the One Ring that Frodo seeks to destroy by casting it into the volcanic furnace at the top of Mt. Doom before it can be regained by Sauron for whom it was forged.

The One Ring was not unique except in its potential. In Eregion long before the tale begins, elven smiths had fashioned three rings for themselves—rings for healing, making and understanding. In addition they had created seven for the dwarf-lords and nine for mortal men. The One Ring, however, could control them all. Unfortunately Sauron had three dwarf rings already in his possession, while four had been eaten by dragons. And the nine mortal men with their rings had so fallen under his spell they had become "ring-wraiths," hollow shadows of their former selves, completely under the sway of the Evil One.

As noted earlier, fairy-tales, flowing as they do out of the unconscious, often reveal in a startling fashion the peculiar spiritual problems that are unresolved in any particular age, along with suggestions for their solution. If this be true, *The Lord of the Rings* would indicate that the spiritual problem par excellence of our time is the *use of power.* The only answer is a willingness to sacrifice it.

One might argue that the handling of personal power has been always man's spiritual dilemma. But Tolkien was writing prior, during and just after World War II in a period when scientific knowledge was increasing by geometric progressions. Nuclear energy, insights into the structure and chemistry of man and nature have magnified the problem of power to a point never before imagined. Theologians once might speak of waging a "just war." Now, with atomic bombs, even small conflicts threaten the entire human race. When a late Archbishop of Canterbury was asked whether he thought God would let man blow up the world, he shocked the press by answering "yes." Moreover, the frightening prospect of one nation or a group of persons possessing enough power to tyrannize the rest of humanity is part of the anxiety of our age. Hence, the One Ring dramatically expresses the collective fears of our time — apprehensions that are no longer unconscious.

Obviously it is not a new question. When the Devil took our Lord up into a high mountain and showed him all the kingdoms of the world and the glory of them and said, "All these I will give you, if you will fall down and worship me" (Mt. 4:9), he was raising the same issue. For it is not just a matter of expanding knowledge but the spiritual question of whom one serves — the God who created us and transcends us or our own personal or collective self-interest. As St. Paul put it:

> For we are not contending against flesh and blood, but against the world rulers of this present darkness, against the spiritual hosts of wickedness in the heavenly places.   (Ephesians 6:12)

The One Ring and Sauron, the Evil One, symbolize all that Paul contends with. As our scientific ability advances, the potential for using it for good or evil likewise is intensified.

It may prove helpful at this point to consider the imagery of the ring itself. A ring has come to mean many things and convey a variety of meanings. On the one hand it is the symbol of wholeness and completeness. The ancients spoke of it as representing God whose center was everywhere and circumference nowhere.

In marriage the ring is a sign of unity — the coupling of two persons, the joining of masculine and feminine as in the Yin-Yang image of Chinese thought.

A Bishop wears a ring not merely to show his union with Christ and the Church but as an outer manifestation of his power and authority.

In the same way a King or nobleman might give his ring to an emissary to indicate that the bearer had his permission to bind him to a promise.

The One Ring incorporates all these meanings. It is the symbol of a god-like potential both to protect its bearer and yet bind him and others to the Master. As the tale indicates, it is safe for a time only in the hands of a very humble creature — in this case a hobbit — who even so becomes more and more possessed by it the more he is forced to use it.

For this is the strange paradox of human power — be it in individuals, families, corporations, churches or government. You must gain power to become adequate and develop a sense of self-worth. Fathers and mothers need power to protect and guide their children. Leaders in industry, schools, churches or government must have authority to act or the result will be chaos. Yet when they exercise power for long, the tendency will be to abuse it — to manipulate and coerce, to dominate and, in the end, use force to maintain control.

Dostoevsky in the memorable "Grand Inquisitor" scene in the *Brothers Karamazov* dramatically portrays the rationale of the Church during the Inquisition, using force to bend unwilling converts to Christ. Jesus returns to Seville and confronts the Grand Inquisitor himself. The old man recognizes the Lord. But he defends his actions because Christ has left mankind free; whereas, according to the Inquisitor, man craves authority, mystery and miracles. Dostoevsky is not denying the place of the organized Church to spread Christ's Kingdom. He does show how the Church gives in to the temptation to use illicit power to achieve these ends.

The One Ring in the Trilogy has the strange quality of turning the bearer invisible each time he uses it. Frodo literally disappears when he places the ring on his finger in desperate situations. Here is symbolized the most demonic aspect of power—that our own self-interest is so often hidden when we use power ostensibly for the benefit of others.

Politicians can talk about "national security" to avoid investigations. Mothers can tell their children they are acting only for "your own good." Behind the mask of benign concern for the well-being of others, untold selfishness can be hidden. The One Ring depicts the subtlety of such manipulations.

A recent characterization of Adolph Hitler appeared as follows:

> To all appearances Hitler was . . . a religious man. In his public speeches he frequently involved the name of the Almighty and Providence. Although not an active churchgoer, he was seen with Protestant and Catholic Church leaders . . . Moreover, Hitler exemplified and inculcated the Victorian virtues of thrift, industry, honesty, courage and love of family and country. He honored motherhood and was constantly pictured as a lover of little children and flowers. He posed as the patron of the arts . . . He restored law and order. He ended unemployment. He built the Volkswagen and the Autobahn. He probably did at least as much for the workers and the poor as any Administration in the U.S.[12]

The very silence of German intelligentsia and Church leaders is indicative of how invisible the real motives of Hitler were to those around him. After all, he was doing his best for the fatherland and the common good.

Even Hitler's actions towards the Jews is reminiscent of the High Priest Caiaphas' admonition, "It is expedient that one man die rather than the nation perish" (cf. John 11:50).

69

Rather the Jews be the scapegoats for any failures than Hitler and his regime.

Again the answer is not that we forego using power. We have to exercise it. But there must be consciousness in ourselves and others about our desire to hang on to it and maintain it for our own ego-needs. The more Frodo uses the Ring, the more he is unwilling or unable to let it go unless forced to do so.

The problem is compounded because the more you seek strength to overthrow tyranny, the greater the tendency to fall into the same trap.

Boromir, one of the companions traveling with Frodo, wants to use the Ring to defend Minas Tirith, but to do so he must take it from him.

'Ah! The Ring!,' said Boromir, his eyes lighting. 'The Ring! . . . Could I not have a sight of it again?'

Frodo looked up. His heart went suddenly cold. He caught the strange gleam in Boromir's eyes, yet his face was still kind and friendly. 'It is best that it should lie hidden,' he answered.

'As you wish. I care not,' said Boromir. 'Yet may I not even speak of it? For you seem ever to think only of its power in the hands of the Enemy: of its evil uses not of its good. The world is changing, you say. Minas Tirith will fall, if the Ring lasts. But why? Certainly, if the Ring were with the Enemy. But why, if it were with us?'[13]

The dictum of Lord Acton that power corrupts and absolute power corrupts asolutely states part of the problem. However, the power must be used, and how it is to be handled is the riddle of the tale.

The answer of the Trilogy is that power can be trusted only in the hands of one who will sacrifice it for the well-being of others.

At the bridge of Khazad-dum, Ganzalf the Grey stands alone against the onrush of the mighty Balrog supported by an army of evil, frenzied orcs.

His enemy halted again, facing him, and the

70

shadow about it reached out like two vast wings. It raised the whip, and the thongs whined and cracked. Fire came from its nostrils. But Gandalf stood firm . . . .

'He cannot stand alone!' cried Aragorn suddenly and ran back along the bridge . . . .

At that moment Gandalf cried aloud and smote the bridge before him. The staff broke asunder and fell from his hand. A blinding sheet of white flame sprang up. The bridge cracked. Right at the Balrog's feet it broke, and the stone upon which it stood crashed into the gulf, while the rest remained, poised, quivering like a tongue of rock thrust out into emptiness.

With a terrible cry the Balrog fell forward, and its shadow plunged down and vanished. But even as it fell it swung its whip, and the thongs lashed and curled about the wizard's knees, dragging him to the brink. He staggered and fell, grasped vainly at the stone, and slid into the abyss. 'Fly, you fools!' he cried, and was gone.[14]

With this offering of self, the party bearing the Ring was saved for the moment and moved forward on their quest. And the words of the Gospel, "Greater love hath no man than he give up his life for his friends," echoes in Gandalf's actions. Moreover, it is significant that the wizard consistently refused to handle the Ring himself for fear that out of pity he would succumb to its spell.

Nevertheless, the ultimate sacrifice of the One Ring itself is accomplished only by a Providence over and beyond them all. Gollum, the slimy creature who once possessed the Ring, bites it off with Frodo's finger, dances like a mad thing, and falls into the volcano. With him the Ring is destroyed. Frodo could not have willed to do this himself. Thereby Tolkien suggests that another mysterious power is at work in the universe without which self-sacrifice is impossible. It is as if Divine Grace is in a polar relationship with Sauron and the One Ring.

There is a strange aspect to the Ring tale which is different from the New Testament, and it is that the destruction of the One Ring causes the other rings to diminish. Tolkien seems to be suggesting that if we are to survive the Evil One in our nuclear age through the self-sacrifice of power, we may find ourselves set back perhaps into a more primitive era. Undoubtedly there are those who have speculated that this may have actually happened to civilizations before.

Nevertheless, at the heart of both the Trilogy and the Christian Gospel the theme is the same: freely offered sacrificial love is at the mysterious center of the universe so that those who offer it are supported by the Grace of God.

The Choosing of the Kingdom

All the council sat with downcast eyes, as if in deep thought. A great dread fell on him (Frodo) as if he was awaiting the pronouncement of some doom that he had long foreseen and vainly hoped might after all never be spoken . . . . At last with an effort he spoke, and wondered to hear his own words, as if some other will was using his small voice.

'I will take the Ring,' he said, 'though I do not know the way.'[15]

The moment Frodo made his decision he became one of the "chosen ones." For the "chosen people" are those who respond to the offer or call of life with conscious decision. Up to this moment Frodo has agreed only to carry the Ring as far as Rivendell, partly to please Gandalf, partly to satisfy his own need for adventure and partly to follow in the steps of his Uncle Bilbo. Now, however, he is the Ring Bearer in deadly earnest, well aware of the dangers that this entails.

The mystery of God's election of Abraham, Moses, David and their decendents is that they responded to God's call by choosing to go along with it. In responding to God's choice, they became the chosen. They chose to be chosen.

Scholars have suggested that the Book of Deuteronomy was written to confront each new generation of Jewish people with the choice of following Yahweh for themselves. It is one thing to be born a Jew; another to be one out of conscious choice. Imaginatively reading Deuteronomy, you stand there before Moses at Mt. Sinai and hear his words directed, not to someone in the dim past, but directly to yourself: "I call heaven and earth to witness against you this day, that I have set before you life and death, blessing and curse; therefore choose life, that you and your descendents may live . . ." (Deut. 30:19).

Of course, if you are a Christian, you have the same problem. Conceivably you were baptized as an infant, have gone through Confirmation as a formality and find yourself like Samwise, loyally following Frodo but only semi-conscious of what this means. Since the days of the Emperor Constantine, conventional or cultural Christianity has been often more of a curse than a blessing. Indeed, Evelyn Frost notes how the healing ministry of the Church diminished when Christianity became the implicit and then official state religion. For all its evil, persecution had made being a Christian a matter of harsh choice. And when this was removed, in Frost's words, a community of saints became instead a group in which saints might be found.

Thus evangelists pressing a decision for Christ always have their place. I will never forget receiving a "decision card" following a Billy Graham Crusade from a man who less than six months before had stood before the Bishop to reconfirm his baptismal vows. "I needed to do it," he told me. "I really meant it this time."

In the same way Samwise does not have a conscious commitment to guard the Ring until at the doors of the Mines of Moria, Gandalf informed him that old Bill, his beloved pony, can go no further with them. Angrily and with bitter tears Sam appears to agree, but when snakes frighten old Bill and grab at Frodo's legs, Sam starts first one way and then the other. In a flash he must decide whether to chase his pony or save Frodo. He rushes to Frodo slashing at the snake with his knife. Later he declares in a choking voice,

> Poor old Bill! . . . Poor old Bill! Wolves and Snakes! . . . I had to choose, Mr. Frodo. I had to come with you.[16]

Sometimes Christians ignore the New Testament witness that our Lord confronted his disciples continually

74

with the need to make choices if they are to follow him. The fishermen must leave their nets, their livelihood, their families. Matthew, the tax collector must walk away from his job. When a scribe approached Jesus saying, "Teacher, I will follow you wherever you go," Jesus reminds him of the perils: "Foxes have holes, and birds of the air have nests; but the Son of man has nowhere to lay his head" (Mt. 8:19, 20). Another asks permission to bury his father, but Jesus replied, ". . . leave the dead to bury their own dead" (Mt. 8:22).

In the past Christians have believed that because a man deliberately chooses not to accept Christ, that person is damned to hell or predestined by God not to believe. This attitude fails to recognize the far worse situation where one does not choose at all, for God can write a choosing person into the divine script far better than one who sits on the fence avoiding any decision.

Take the case of the rich young man who asked Jesus what he lacked. He was told to sell what he possessed, give to the poor and follow our Lord. The young man turned away sorrowing because he had great possessions (Mt. 19:16-20). *Yet he made a choice.* And I suspect his choice not to follow Christ has led more people to make a conscious decision for Christ than any other episode in the New Testament.

I will never forget hearing the poet, T.S. Eliot, tell how he became a Christian. It seems that he had spent some time listening to confirmed atheist Bertrand Russell read his latest diatribe against Christianity. The attack so nauseated Eliot that he went into the first Anglican church he could find and fell down on his knees. Without the atheist Russell, there might have been no Christian Eliot.

Now choice is the exerciae of free will in selecting one alternative over another. There is no choice, for example, if we merely acquiesce or go along when we are afraid or don't want to be bothered. When a politician says, "I do not choose to run," he is doing just that. Other forces are making the decision for him. Thus at a critical moment on Mt. Doom, Frodo is so possessed by the Ring that he cannot throw it into the volcano after coming all that tortuous way to do that very thing.

'I have come,' he (Frodo) said. 'But I do not choose now to do what I came to do.'[17]

In her provocative treatise, "Choice in the Lord of the Rings," Helen Luke writes:

> A conscious choice must spring from the clearest possible discrimination of the issues involved. We must listen to reason and common sense, we must recognize, bring to consciousness our desire and fears and only then will we be able to hear the verdict of the heart. For if anything stands out more clearly . . . it is that right choices spring always from the heart—the word used to mean not the seat of the emotions, but the place where the cold intellect and hot desires meet, are honored and then unite in true objective feeling.[18]

After being threatened, chased and wounded on the road to Rivendell while carrying the Ring, Frodo is far more ready to make a conscious choice to bear it further than he was before. The same can be said for our Lord's disciples following his Crucifixion and Resurrection. Any illusions of what it meant to be his disciple were dissipated.

One of the surer tests that you have made a "conscious" decision is your willingness to accept the consequences, good and bad, of the choice you have made. It is significant that St. Paul, while citing all his hardships, never complains about them; in fact, he makes his boast in them:

> Five times I have received at the hands of the Jews the forty lashes less one. Three times I have been beaten with rods; once I was stoned. Three times I have been shipwrecked; a night and a day I have been adrift at sea; on frequent journeys, in danger from rivers, danger from robbers, danger from my own people, in danger from Gentiles, danger in the city, danger in the wilderness, danger at sea, danger from false brethren; in toil and hardship, through many a sleepless night, in hunger and thirst, often without food, in cold and exposure. And, apart from other things, there is

the daily pressure upon me of my anxiety for all the churches. (2 Cor. 11:24-28).

The more unconscious our decisions, the more we blame people, circumstances or ourselves.

No choice is irrevocable; further choices always follow the initial one, but you accept what befalls you when you have consciously made the decision. Often our choices will have been misguided or mistaken. But the Divine Life at the center of the universe seemingly is able to use even our poorest when we have chosen from the heart.

The tendancy is always to avoid such *personal* decisions. Pontius Pilate washes his hands of any personal verdict when he complies with the cry of the crowd, "His blood be on us and on our children." Here is a no-decision from both — Pilate denying that the choice was his, and the crowd saying "on us" rather than "on me." In the Trilogy Boromir speaking about himself says, "The men of Minas Tirith are true to their word," rather than, "I am true to my word." It's frightening to make decisions and own the results.

The choice Jesus offers you and me is deciding for or against the Kingdom of God rather than for or against himself.

If I am not doing the works of my Father, then do not believe me; but if I do them, even though you do not believe me, believe the works, that you may know and understand that the Father is in me and I am in the Father. (John 10:37, 38)

This is why at times you can apparently be against Christianity and yet be for the Kingdom of God within you. Despite the Gospel warnings that we are to allow God to be the final judge of who are Christian and who are not, who are in the Kingdom and who are not, we tend to want stereotyped Christian responses. A man once told me that a priest with whom he was taking instruction into the Church told him that the Church had a tailor-made suit for him to fit into. He had just to take it off the rack and put it on. The man felt far more unique than this and walked away from Christ and the Church for another twenty years. Rightly or wrongly he believed he would violate something profound and deep within himself if he had become a Christian at that time. However, he had not consciously chosen the Kingdom until he had again assessed his relationship to Christ. For, while Christ and the Kingdom of God may be intellectually separated, still Jesus is the dramatic, personal manifestation of the Kingdom's reality in human life. To consciously accept Jesus as the Christ is also to choose to live in the Kingdom of God in this world.

I was reading recently from a biography of C.S. Lewis, who in 1916 wrote his friend Arnold Greeves, while in Oxford: "All religions, that is all mythologies, to give them their proper name, are merely man's own invention—Christ as much as Loki."

If you read Lewis' childhood experience with a psychotic headmaster and clergyman, you can understand that emotionally as well as intellectually he might say this out of the inner integrity of his own experience.

In 1929 he says in his book, *Surprised by Joy*:

> That which I greatly feared had at last come upon me. In Trinity term of 1929 I gave in, and admitted that God was God and knelt and prayed, perhaps, that night the most dejected and reluctant convert in England. I did not even see what is now the most shining and obvious thing; the Divine humility which will accept a convert even on such terms.[19]

Christians need the same humility to accept people who may reject Christ outwardly for the sake of an integrity within them. Personally, I would like everyone to choose Jesus as their Lord from the heart. But rather than be half-hearted Christians, I'd rather they reject him and choose not to follow him. Such persons, I am convinced, are closer to God than wishy-washy Christians. Dimly I hear the late Gert Behanna thanking God that before her conversion she wasn't one of those sniveling sinners but a wholehearted one.[20] The last thing the Church needs is apologetic, half-hearted Christians.

If this thesis is correct, that the chosen people are those who consciously choose in response to life-situations, it may well be that many are choosing the Kingdom without connecting their decisions with Jesus Christ at all. However, if Jesus is the true manifestation of the Kingdom of God in human form, to choose the Kingdom is to bring one into the dimension of Reality where he is to be found. Conversely, to wholeheartedly relate yourself to Christ is to enter the Kingdom which flows through him.

In either case this does not mean that "the chosen people" are thereby morally superior to anyone else. When you look at the Hebrew people following Moses or the motley crew who are disciples of our Lord, it is reminiscent of a statement attributed to the Duke of Wellington reviewing his troops: "I don't know what they'll do to the enemy," he is said to have commented, "but they frighten me to death."

Along the same line Frodo says to Gandalf,

> 'I am not made for perilous quests. I wish I had never seen the Ring! Why did it come to me? Why was I chosen?'
>
> 'Such questions cannot be answered,' said Gandalf. 'You may be sure that it was not for any merit that others do not possess: not for power or wisdom at any rate . . . 'the decision lies with you . . . . I will help you bear this burden, as long as it is yours to bear.'[21]

Gandalf's words state the case. It is a matter of consciously choosing and accepting the consequences rather than virtue that creates the "chosen ones." And even when you choose, it is possible to err; but it is as by walking with Gandalf or Christ that you are enabled to bear that burden.

Some may understandably object that "to choose is to be chosen" hardly expresses what the Gospels have to say. Jesus expressly tells his disciples, "You did not choose me, but I chose you . . ." (John 15:16). The same thing could be said about Abraham, or Moses or David. But if you distinguish between the opportunities and your own response, it makes sense of our Lord's other statement: "For many are called, but few are chosen" (Mt. 22:14). The fact is that Jesus invites the multitude (everyone) to repent and enter into the Kingdom of God, but only a few respond to him. Consistently in other areas of life this is true as well, be it business, art, writing, politics or military actions. Those who consciously choose are the chosen.

The Christian Gospel is then coherent with all aspects of life where awareness and decision bring the prize. Jesus makes you conscious of the presence of God in you and around you by manifesting this presence in and through himself. When, in the Trilogy, Theoden is freed by Gandalf from the demonic influence of Wormtongue, he then is able to act decisively against the evil tide rising around him. So when by the grace of God you are liberated from the unconscious stupor that would keep you from decision in whatever area of your life, you have then tasted of the Kingdom that Jesus Christ reveals.

The chosen people then are those who choose when confronted by the call of life. What is at stake is the Kingdom of God within us and among us, recognized or not. The more conscious your choices, the more you are drawn into the center of that divine plan and mystery that permeates your life.

PART III
THE CHRONICLES OF
NARNIA

The Chronicles of Narnia

The credibility of fairy tales as a vehicle for communicating Christian truth has been immensely enhanced by the writings of C.S. Lewis in his seven *Chronicles of Narnia*. This series is far more self-consciously Christian than Tolkien's *The Lord of the Rings*. "Narnia" is that realm into which the Pevensie children walk through a wardrobe closet and where they encounter Aslan, the Lion—the Christ figure of that region.

At the conclusion of *The Voyage of the Dawntreader*, Lucy Pevensie says to Aslan:

"Before we go, will you tell us when we can come back to Narnia again? Please."

"Dearest," said Aslan very gently, "you and your brother will never come back to Narnia."

"Oh, *Aslan!*" said Edmund and Lucy both together in despairing voices . . . .

"It isn't Narnia, you know," sobbed Lucy. "It's *you*. We shan't meet *you* there. And how can we live, never meeting you?"

"But you shall meet me, dear one." said Aslan.

"Are—are you there too, Sir?" said Edmund.

"I am," said Aslan. "But there I have another name. You must learn to know me by that name. This was the very reason why you were brought to Narnia, that by knowing me here for a little, you may know me better there."[22]

With this intention in mind, the following three chapters will reflect upon three incidents out of the Narnia tales that present elements from the Gospels in a fresh and disarming way.

Breaking the Witch's Spell

The good news of the New Testament is that the life, death and resurrection of Jesus Christ have released us from our slavery to sin and the resulting consequences of death.

Over and over we sing, "The strife is o'er, the battle done, the victory of life is won." And yet do we believe this affirmation? What was so clear in the mind of Paul and the early evangelists has become so often a vague, abstract idea as it trickles down the centuries to us. Somehow we need to relive the dramatic events which free us from our prison of sin and fear of death.

In *The Lion, the Witch and the Wardrobe* Lewis provides such an opportunity.

According to the tale, the four Pevensie children have walked into Narnia through a wardrobe closet and discovered a country under the evil spell of the White Witch. The atmosphere is cold. Frost and snow are in the air.

One of the four children is a spoiled little boy named Edmund. He is selfish, likes to tease, and is painful to have around.

Edmund is the first to encounter the White Witch and immediately falls under her enchantment. She promises him Turkish Delight and a high office in her realm if he will tell her where the other children can be found. In addition to these enticements Edmund is acutely aware of a dangerous force lurking behind her friendly overtures. Indeed,

85

with a wave of her wand the White Witch can turn anyone she dislikes into a stone statue—a capacity with which she can frighten almost anyone into doing her will. So when the opportunity arises, Edmund, like Judas, informs the Witch that his brother and sisters are at the Beaver's house. By so doing he places himself fully in the Witch's power.

Then a strange thing happens. The air becomes warmer. The snow begins to melt. Tidings come that Aslan, the great Lion and savior of Narnia, is returning. The White Witch and her followers are thrown into paroxysms of fear. Nonetheless, she goes out to meet Aslan demanding the right to execute Edmund at the stone altar, for according to the law of the land, any betrayer belongs to her and anyone in her power she has the right to kill.

At this point Aslan offers to take the place of Edmund himself. The White Witch and her minions are stunned beyond belief. Yet while Edmund snivels in the background and his brother and sisters watch in horror, Aslan gives himself over to the hideous designs of the White Witch. Here is the scene from Lewis' tale.

A howl and a gibber of dismay went up from the creatures when they first saw the great Lion pacing towards them, and for a moment the Witch herself seemed to be struck with fear. Then she recovered herself and gave a wild, fierce laugh.

"The fool!" she cried. "The fool has come. Bind him fast."

. . . The hags made a dart at him and shrieked with triumph when they found that he made no resistance at all. Then others—evil dwarfs and apes—rushed in to help them and between them they rolled the huge Lion round on his back and tied all his four paws together . . . . Then they began to drag him towards the Stone Table.

"Stop!" said the Witch. "Let him first be shaved."

Another roar of mean laughter went up from her followers as an ogre with a pair of shears came forward and squatted down by Aslan's head. Snip-snip-snip went the shears and masses of curling gold began to fall to the ground. Then the ogre stood back and the children, watching from their hiding-place, could see the face of Aslan looking all small and different without its mane. The enemies also saw the difference.

"Why, he's only a great cat after all!" cried one.

"Is *that* what we were afraid of?" said another.

And they surged round Aslan jeering at him, saying things like "Puss, Puss! Poor Pussy," and "How many mice have you caught today, Cat?" and "Would you like a saucer of milk, Pussums?" . . . .

When once Aslan had been tied (and tied so that he was really a mass of cords) on the flat stone, a hush fell on the crowd. Four Hags, holding four torches, stood at the corners of the Table. The Witch bared her arms as she had bared them the previous night when it had been Edmund instead of Aslan. Then she began to whet her knife . . . .

At last she drew near. She stood by Aslan's head. Her face was working and twitching with passion, but his looked up at the sky, still quiet, neither angry nor afraid, but a little sad. Then, just before she gave the blow, she stooped down and said in a quivering voice,

"And now, who has won? Fool, did you think that by all this you would save the human traitor? Now I will kill you instead of him as our pact was and so the Deep Magic will be appeased. But when you are dead what will prevent me from killing him as well? And who will take him out of my hand *then*? Understand that you have given me Narnia forever, you have lost your own life and you have not saved his. In that knowledge, despair and die."[23]

Briefly, such is the story, but it is enlightening to reflect upon the symbolism with which Lewis embellishes and tells his tale.

Take the White Witch, for example. She is evil personified. She enslaves others by appealing to their selfish motives on the one hand and to their fears on the other.

As a woman and a witch, she represents feminine values become demonic. It is our motherly nurturing side that is concerned for adequate food, protection, harmony and peace. But the White Witch uses these legitimate concerns for her own ends. She offers them to silence any opposition—to turn critics into stone. She immobilizes those who might stand against her by her seeming goodness. She is a "White" Witch cloaking her evil intentions by providing food to eat, fighting unnecessary battles, backing law and order with cruel strength. She is no different from some sadistic parent obscuring tyranny under the guise of benign love.

Hence, Edmund is offered sweets, status in her Kingdom and the implied promise that she will stand behind him with her power. Here on another level are the classic temptations of Christ to use food or stardom or worldly power to spread the Kingdom of God. The White Witch is Satan in Narnian form. Edmund succumbs, whereas our Lord resisted.

The White Witch is unmasked and her strength broken only when Aslan personally comes upon the scene, sacrificing himself for Edmund and the others who are petrified by the Witch's spell. To paraphrase Paul, sin and death are overcome when one in the form of God empties himself, becomes obedient unto death and offers himself as a sacrifice for us. Only in the brilliant light of such love are we made conscious of the Evil One working in our midst, among leaders of Church and State, the collective mental-ity of the crowd, in the moral and pious and in the follower-sof the Son of God themselves.

In New Testament terms, Satan (the White Witch) must be driven from heaven—become visible and disconnected from God—before he/she can be conquered (Luke 10:18, Rev. 12:1-7).

Yet consciousness is not sufficient in itself. To be aware of our chains and cells is one thing, but God must act to get us out. Aslan must come in actuality, put himself under the Witch's power and truly die before the evil magic is destroyed.

Christianity is not just knowledge, teaching or height-ened awareness. It takes a concrete, actual event—a real and totally loving sacrifice—to release the Holy Spirit into the lives of people imprisoned by sin in its various dimensions.

88

Here is indeed a mystery. When Aslan (or Christ) offers himself for us, a deeper magic which goes back beyond the dawn of time is constellated. Sin is exposed; its power broken; its consequences (death) nullified. Those in Christ (Aslan) are given not only an awareness that evil may hide behind white facades but the courage to stand against it in the knowledge that Satan has been decisively beaten. Christians face death with the understanding that God will resurrect them through death but not protect them from it.

So does Lewis re-state the Passion narrative, enriching the Gospel with a fairy tale in order that you and I may respond as if we were encountering the story for the first time.

It can be argued that Lewis is wrong, that the White Witch is not dead but very much alive in our sinful, hate-filled world—cast out of Narnia perhaps, but not from earth. Yet surely the New Testament does proclaim Satan's or the White Witch's decisive defeat. Moreover, even when an enemy has lost and its leaders fallen, its prisoners must still be released. Nor is it unusual for enemy troops to battle on and on in a fanatical, fruitless attempt to win a war that can't be won.

How Eustace Was Changed

"There was a boy called Eustace Clarence Scrubb, and he almost deserved it." So begins *The Voyage of the Dawntreader*. As you might guess, much of the book concerns how Eustace was transformed, first into a dragon and then back into being human.

Eustace was a cousin of the Pevensie children and heartily disliked them. The feeling was mutual. And when all of them ended up on King Caspian's ship in Narnia sailing towards the end of the world, it was not surprising that Eustace created problems from the start. He began by crying copiously and then complaining angrily. Next, he picked on the knightly mouse, Reepicheep, only to come out the loser. Finally, to get out of work, he wandered away, became lost and fell asleep in a dead dragon's lair with all its hoard of treasure (which Eustace naturally wanted to claim all for himself). What happened was astonishing, but as Lewis says, only to those who read all the wrong books. Eustace became a dragon. Sleeping on a dragon's hoard with greedy dragonish thoughts in his heart, Eustace became a serpentine monster with smoke coming out of his nostrils, complete with wings and forelegs. Now he was cut off from the human race. It made him wonder if he had really been the nice person he had thought himself to be. And in his loneliness he longed for the company of those whom he had treated with so little consideration or regard.

For the first time, but now as a full-fledged dragon, Eustace volunteered to help the crew of the Dawntreader in every way he could.

"Well, anyway, I looked up and saw the very last thing I expected: a huge lion coming slowly towards me. And one queer thing was that there was no moon last night, but there was moonlight where the lion was . . . . I was terribly afraid of it. You may think that, being a dragon, I could have knocked any lion out easily enough. But it wasn't that kind of fear. I wasn't afraid of it eating me, I was just afraid of *it*—if you can understand. Well, it came closer up to me and looked straight into my eyes. And I shut my eyes tight. But that wasn't any good because it told me to follow it."

"You mean it spoke?"

"I don't know. Now that you mention it, I don't think it did . . . . And I knew I'd have to do what it told me, so I got up and followed it. And it led me a long way into the mountains. And there was always this moonlight over and round the lion wherever we went. So at last we came to the top of a mountain I'd never seen before and on the top of this mountain there was a garden—trees and fruit and everything. In the middle of it there was a well.

". . . The water was as clear as anything and I thought if I could get in there and bathe it would ease the pain in my leg. But the lion told me I must undress first . . . .

"I was just going to say that I couldn't undress because I hadn't any clothes on when I suddenly thought that dragons are snaky sort of things and snakes can cast their skins . . . . So I started scratching myself and my scales began coming off all over the place. And then I scratched a little deeper and, instead of just scales coming off here and there, my whole skin started peeling off beautifully, like it does after an illness, or as if I was a banana. In a minute or two I just stepped out of it . . . . So I started to go down into the well for my bath.

"But just as I was going to put my foot into the water I looked down and saw that it was all hard and rough and wrinkled and scaly just as it had been before. . . . So I scratched and tore again and this under skin peeled off beautifully and out I stepped and left it lying beside the other one and went down to the well for my bath.

91

"Well, exactly the same thing happened again. And I thought to myself, oh dear, how ever many skins have I got to take off? . . . .

"Then the lion said—but I don't know if it spoke— You will have to let me undress you. I was afraid of his claws, I can tell you, but I was pretty nearly desperate now. So I just lay flat down on my back to let him do it.

"The very first tear he made was so deep that I thought it had gone right into my heart. And when he began pulling the skin off, it hurt worse than anything I've ever felt . . . .

"Well, he peeled the beastly stuff right off—just as I thought I'd done it myself the other three times, only they hadn't hurt . . . . And there was I as smooth and soft as a peeled switch and smaller than I had been. Then he caught hold of me . . . and threw me into the water. It smarted like anything but only for a moment. After that it became perfectly delicious.

"After a bit the lion took me out and dressed me—"

"Dressed you. With his paws?"

"Well, I don't exactly remember that bit . . . . Which is what makes me think it must have been a dream."

"No. It wasn't a dream," said Edmund.

"Why not?"

"Well, there are the clothes, for one thing. And you have been—well, un-dragoned, for another."[24]

If you look at what happened to Eustace through the eyes and imagery of the New Testament, you might say he was experiencing a type of baptism, putting off the old man and becoming a new creature in Christ Jesus (2 Cor. 5:17).

Interestingly, Aslan comes to get him. The initiative is with God. You and I rarely want to change until we are almost forced to do so by inner pressure or outer circumstance. Eustace had to see what kind of person he's become, feel wretched about it (be convicted of sin) before Aslan could reach him. Any transformation called for a power beyond himself.

Identifying Eustace's ordeal and healing with Christian

baptism was easier to comprehend in the early Church. In those days candidates underwent a long period of testing, instruction, self-examination, fasting and prayer before their presentation. At the time of their baptism the catechumens confessed their sins, renounced their past loyalties, received absolution, were immersed in water, signed with the sign of the cross and clothed in white robes symbolizing their new life in Christ. Even then baptism was merely the beginning of their Christian adventure, the start of a journey in which the one who loses his / her life will find it (Mt. 10:39).

In our day we think it necessary for people overcoming alcoholism or drug addiction to go through a similar process—but not necessarily the ordinary church member.

Some years ago psychiatrist Fritz Kunkel characterized the neurotic, ego-centered person in four categories as *Star, Turtle, Clinging Vine* and *Nero*. The Star desires to be the center of attention; Turtle hides behind a shell; Clinging Vine clings tenaciously to various dependencies; Nero attempts to dominate through intimidation or force.

If you don't see yourself as a dragon, perhaps one of Kunkel's types will do. None of these attitudes are easy to break, and Christians are not immune from any one of them.

Many of us today are baptized as infants. Yet whether we are children or adults, the sacrament of baptism signifies more than it immediately effects. Baptized as we are into the death and resurrection of Christ, we too will be called to grow in the Spirit by dying to our egocentric nature before we can rise to an ever-expanding self. Eustace's condition is not much different from our own. Christ (Aslan) takes us through death in order that we may be human and alive.

It is significant that Eustace shares his story initially with Edmund, a conscious fellow sinner who will understand. Edmund, of course, had betrayed his brother and sisters into the hand of the White Witch. He knew he had been saved by Aslan just as did Eustace. In addition to a power beyond ourselves, all of us need a group of Christians who will affirm our experience and support us along the way. It is far easier to confide your dark and seamier side to one who has faced his own shadow than to those who see themselves as morally upright and pure. Edmund can be a confessor because he has known the absolving, forgiving reality of Aslan for himself. As he reminds Eustace, he was a traitor and Eustace merely an ass.

Most importantly, both have discovered the unconditional, unmerited grace-giving love of God. Such knowledge— a gift to the repentant—still leaves them with a mystery. Aslan is not a tame lion but an elusive saviour.

"Who is Aslan? Do you know him?" asks Eustace of Edmund.

"Well—he knows me." Edmund replies, telling it as it is.[25]

On Being Taken In
and Taken Out

In the final book of the Chronicles of Narnia, *The Last Battle*, there is a chapter with the intriguing title, "How the Dwarfs Refused to Be Taken In."

The dwarfs in the tale, led on by Griffle, had been tricked by an ape, named Shift, into believing in a false Aslan, a donkey dressed in a lion's skin. The make-believe Aslan had ordered the dwarfs to become slaves of the Calormenes. They were dutifully following some Calormene soldiers when they were rescued by King Tirian, Jill and Eustace. But having been taken in once by a false Aslan, the dwarfs now refused to believe in Aslan at all. "Dwarfs are for dwarfs" became their motto.

Later the same dwarfs are a part of a group of Narnian skeptics standing before a stable door. The ape tells the doubting assembly that they can meet the Calormene god, "Tash," by going through the door one at a time. Of course, all are warned that should they go through the stable door, they are in danger of being comsumed by Tash. The whole scenario is a staged plot because behind the door lurks a Calormene soldier ready to strike down any courageous Narnian with his sword.

By this time, no matter what happens (and much does), the dwarfs refuse to believe or follow any god, be it Tash or Aslan. When a battle ensues between the Calormenes and Narnians, the Dwarfs shoot their arrows at both sides, shouting, "The dwarfs are for the dwarfs." When they are captured and thrown through the stable door by the Calormenes, a strange thing occurs. Whereas the followers of Aslan who go through it discover a wonderful land filled with flowers, fruit and sunlight, the dwarfs experience that other side as a dark stable filled with straw. When Lucy tries to help them see and make them aware of what is around them, the dwarfs are unable to respond. The flowers she puts before them smell like stable litter. Even when the real Aslan appears, all but the dwarfs are overjoyed to see him. The fact is they are not aware of him at all.

"Aslan," said Lucy through her tears, "could you —will you—do something for these poor Dwarfs?"

"Dearest," said Aslan, "I will show you both what I can, and what I cannot, do." He came close to the Dwarfs and gave a long growl: low, but it set all the air shaking. But the Dwarfs said to one another, "Hear that? That's the gang at the other end of the Stable. Trying to frighten us . . . ."

Aslan raised his head and shook his mane. Instantly a glorious feast appeared on the Dwarfs' knees: pies and tongues and pigeons and trifles and ices, and each Dwarf had a goblet of good wine in his right hand. But it wasn't much use. They began eating and drinking greedily enough, but it was clear that they couldn't taste it properly. They thought they were eating and drinking only the sort of things you might find in a Stable . . . .

"You see," said Aslan. "They will not let us help them. They have chosen cunning instead of belief. Their prison is only in their own minds, yet they are in that prison; and so afraid of being taken in that they can not be taken out."[26]

The situation of the dwarfs for readers of the Narnia stories was not unlike selfish old Uncle Andrew in *The Magician's Nephew* who was unable to understand the voice of Aslan, hearing only growlings and roars.

Lewis is thus suggesting that people may not be aware of the presence of Jesus Christ or who he is despite the most obvious signs—*that seeing is not believing. Rather, believing enables one to see.*

In the 20th chapter of the Gospel of John, Thomas is not with the other disciples when the risen Christ appears to them. When the others tell him they have seen the Lord, Thomas replies, "Unless I see in his hands the print of the nails, and place my finger in the mark of the nails, and place my hand in his side, I will not believe" (John 20:25)

Eight days later Thomas was with the other disciples when Jesus suddenly stood in their midst. He said to Thomas,

> "Put your finger here, and see my hands; and put out your hand, and place it in my side; do not be faithless, but believing." Thomas answered him, "My Lord and my God!" Jesus said to him, "Have you believed because you have seen me? Blessed are those who have not seen and yet believe."
>
> (John 20:27-29)

With this question the Gospel of John reaches its crescendo, for throughout the evangelist's account, people have time and time again seen and not believed either that a miracle had occurred or that Jesus was the Christ. Some cannot see the sign. Others see the wonder but are unaware that God is in Christ.

At the wedding in Cana, water is turned into wine, but the comment by the steward of the feast was that usually people serve the best wine first but here they have kept the good wine until now (John 2:10).

A blind man is touched by Christ and regains his sight, but even he has great difficulty in accepting Jesus for who he is. The leading churchmen of that day, the Pharisees, refused to accept that a healing had even occurred.

A multitide were involved in the feeding of the five thousand. Yet in their minds Jesus was merely a wonder-worker whom they wished to make an earthly King. The reality of God's Kingdom remains hidden from their eyes.

In the New Testament as in Lewis' tale, Jesus as the Christ appears only to those who are already close to him, for the faith-seeing of belief cannot be forced. If Thomas had not loved Jesus—he had been willing to risk death in following him (John 11:16)—either he would not have been aware of the risen Christ, or like the dwarfs he would have assumed it was some trick.

Presumably, if Jesus had approached Pilate or Caiaphas after his resurrection they, too, would have been so afraid of being taken in they would not have been able to be taken out. Paul may seem to be an exception; but his experience with the dying Stephen, no doubt, had brought him nearer to belief than he consciously imagined.

Unlike the dwarfs with Aslan, Thomas believed and hence can see, not merely the resurrected Lord in the room among them (the sign) but that Jesus is the Christ (what the sign means). "My Lord and my God," he exclaims.

It is always a question, then, whether you or I are more like Thomas or the cunning dwarfs. St. John's Gospel and the fairy tale confront us with the same choice. Are we so afraid of being taken in that we cannot be taken out into the Kingdom of God?

Our final assurance is that there is a great blessing for those who have not seen and yet believe. For such persons are like Thomas before his encounter with the risen Lord. They are already in the Kingdom whether they know it or not, and they will discover signs of its reality around them and all about.

PART IV
WRITING YOUR OWN
FAIRY TALES

Writing Your Own Fairy Tales

The spiritual exercise of writing your own fairy tales is not a highly developed art among Christians. However, if such a practice in active imagination will make you more aware of the Kingdom of God within you, it is well worth doing.

Deep within you and all of us there is a desire for another realm, a longing for something you have dimly experienced but which is ever beyond your reach. Somehow the writing of your own fairy tale— which starts from anywhere, bubbles up from unknown depths and ends in a complete surprise—gives expression and visibility to this inner mystery. It is the world where time has no beginning and no end, and it speaks of God in this indirect and oblique fashion.

If you will recall (Introduction), Tolkien spoke of the values of fantasy, escape, recovery or consolation that are fundamental to fairy tales. When you allow these elements to be spontaneously expressed, something positive transpires within your soul. You discover that you, too, can build secondary worlds out of the very stuff that lies within you. By so doing you become the "sub-creator" of whom Tolkien also speaks—one who has the joy of creating something new from what was not yet there before.

You will further find that although your characters may be blocked by impossible barriers or imprisoned behind impenetrable walls, you have inside of you remarkable capacities to work out of such dilemmas, even as Tolkien suggests.

These considerations are not offered to equate the

Kingdom of God simply with the potential in our unconscious side. However, it is of great value to realize that God is found and works within as well as from without. In addition, as you write your tale, you will be removing or at least revealing some of the unwitting road blocks to the realization of the Kingdom within, since the fairy tale will be expressing symbolically the problems and their possible solutions. And what seems impossible or unrealistic in the outer world is everyday stuff in the realm of the Spirit where, with God, nothing is impossible.

I can hear some hard-headed rationalists saying to themselves, "Oh, come on now. This is the land of make-believe." But I am not talking here simply of a tale you will spin out rationally with conscious thought. You are to relax, prayerfully be in the presence of God, and *let* the story out of you—one you have never dreamed before.

Before me as I am writing is a potted plant. My fairy tale could begin simply:

> Once upon a time there lived in the earth around a large fern a small creature by the name of Ignatius, a bug of a very special religious order that has as its highest aim in life the care and nurture of plant life. And although the order normally labored in community as most religious orders do, Ignatius had been left alone to guard this fern from its enemies because of a particularly ferocious fern attack by hordes of squeasels in another section of that country. So it was that Ignatius was ill-prepared one night when a group of fern-eating squeasels stealthily made their way through the dirt and ground that surrounded the fern and in which it had its life . . . etc."

O.K., there is the plot. Ignatius has been left to guard the fern. Squeasels are all around him threatening both him and the fern. How will he handle this impending disaster? But I am sure, since Ignatius is religious, he will have the faith that all things are possible with God and something will transform the situation. The moment you discover that with you are resources to bring a happy ending out of the most hopeless predicament, you are also in

102

the realm of the New Testament with its confident faith in the power of God.

A year ago I was lecturing at a conference on this subject and discovered that few if any had ever written their own fairy tales, and many were dubious that they could. I had briefed them on my outlook on such an exercise and proceeded to tell them that they all had it in them to write a delightful tale if they would just take the leap and begin. And they all did! Moreover, they were amazed at what came out. After the session, they turned their efforts over to me and suggested I author a book of modern fairy tales. This reaction shows how enthusiastic you can quickly become about your untapped creativity. Here are two of those stories.

The Tale of a Tail

Once upon a time there was a preacher who lost his voice. Not completely, you understand. He could still talk, although he sounded like Jimmy Durante with laryngitis. But he lost his singing voice. He couldn't sing a note anymore. And this discouraged him very much because he liked to sing. He liked to sing at home. He liked to sing in Church. But every time he opened his mouth to sing, the noise came out hoarse and gruff and monotone.

He went to the doctor. The doctor examined his throat and gave him some medicine and said, "Take this for five days and if that doesn't do it, call me and we'll try something else." After five days, he still couldn't sing. But rather than go back to the doctor, he went to his old mother who lived by the sea in a tiny cabin way off in Hawaii.

"Mother," the preacher said, "I have lost my singing voice, and I can no longer lead the songs in Church. If I don't soon get my voice back, I'll lose my job. And besides, it's no fun not to be able to sing at home in the shower or around the house anymore. What shall I do?"

"Son," his old mother said, "Let's try two things. One old remedy and one brand new one. The old remedy is to eat lemon and honey and shut up for three days—just listen. The new remedy is to go deep-sea diving."

The son said to his mother, "I can understand the lemon-honey and keeping my mouth shut, and I will do that. But I surely don't know how deep-sea diving will help."

"Son," his mother said, "You'll see. Or better yet, you'll be singing."

So for three days the preacher ate lemon-honey and shut up. On the morning of the fourth day he still didn't have his voice, so he went out and rented some diving equipment and hired a boat with guide and went out to sea.

He put his diving gear on and started down—fifty feet, seventy-five feet, one hundred feet. All of a sudden he heard a mournful song. To be sure, it was singing, but sad. So he swam toward the sound.

Imagine his surprise when he saw a whale with his tail caught in a big net singing a sad, sad song. It went something like this:

Nobody knows the trouble I'm in—
Not even Jesus.
Nobody knows the trouble I'm in—
With my tail caught in this net.

So the preacher said, in a gruff and growly voice, "Well, you've got your trouble, but at least you can sing."

The whale said, "Well, not much longer. Because if I don't get released from this net very soon, I'll drown. I need air too, just like you."

The preacher said, "What can I do to help?"

The whale said, "You can cut my tail loose."

The preacher said, "How do I know you won't swallow me whole?"

The whale said, "You don't. You'll have to trust me."

So the preacher cut the net loose. And just as he cut the final strands, the whale flipped his tail and shoved the preacher to a spot right in front of the whale's mouth.

The whale started to smile. And he opened his mouth very, very wide. And the whale jumped at the preacher, and the preacher screamed a high C. And he was just barely

able to stay in front of the whale as they both surfaced.
The preacher had the crew pull him into the boat. As he lay there, all pooped, he saw the whale sunning himself, lying on his back smiling.

He said to the whale, "Hey, that wasn't very nice, was it: you frightening me like that?"

The whale replied, "Well, it got you your singing voice back, didn't it?"

And the preacher started to hum, "Praise God . . . ." And the whale smiled. And the preacher sang, "Out of the depth."

■ ■ ■

The Discarded Chair

There once was a chair that was never used or sat upon because it had become so old and decrepit. It was shoved into a corner, and now and then the people who lived in the house would look at it and say, "One day soon we must take that old chair and throw it into the dump."

When they said that, the old chair would shudder and feel more frail than it really was. But the thing that bothered the chair most of all was that when friends would gather for parties and conversation in the home all the other chairs were used. Indeed, the people would sit on the floor rather than touch the old worn-out chair in the corner.

One night, when the old chair was in the deepest kind of depression because it was unnoticed, untouched, unused and unwanted, a strange-looking creature entered through a tiny hole in the floor, looked this way and that, and approached the old chair in the corner. It said, "My, you look so sad and lonely, old chair. Hasn't anyone sat in you lately?" (Obviously you must know that this tiny creature was a "Homer," for the Homer is the only one of God's creatures who can communicate with a chair.)

"Oh, you don't know how glad I am to see you," sobbed

the old chair. The other chairs won't have anything to do with me, and no Homer has passsed this way in years.

"I understand," replied the Homer. "As a matter of fact the Lord Homer asked me to stop by because he sensed you were in a terrible state."

"What can you do to help me?" exclaimed the chair. "Some might find me valuable as an antique, but folks here just see me as a wobbly, unsightly old chair."

"Count on me," said the Homer. "You need to be found by someone who appreciates all you have to give." And with that he disappeared suddenly through the hole in the floor.

The man in the yellow muffler, who stopped by the house the next day to ring the door bell, was puzzled at how he could have ever lost his way. He never realized that while he was driving his car, a Homer had slipped in at the service station when he stopped for gas. Homers, of course, have the power to lead you to one home or another.

"I've lost my way," said the man to the lady of the house. And then he spied the old chair. "Why, you have what I've been looking for," he cried. "Would you sell that chair to me?"

"That old chair!" said the surprised woman. "Is it valuable? We were going to throw it away."

"Valuable to me," answered the man in the yellow muffler.

"If it is that valuable, I'd rather not sell it but fix it up myself," thought the woman.

And that is why the old chair was refinished and repaired. Indeed, it became the central object of furniture in the entire house.

"See this chair," she would tell her friends. "It's the most precious object in our house."

■ ■ ■

Each of these fairy tales took no more than twenty-five to thirty minutes to write. The material seemed to flow like water from an open faucet. Moreover, the person writing discovered a sense of freedom and release which he or she thoroughly enjoyed. In fact, on my desk are two sets of fairy tales by men who continued this form of meditation long after the first experiment had ended.

It is well over a half century since Glenn Clark suggested that our deepest prayers are "soul-sincere desires" of which we are not always conscious.[27] Tolkien also affirms that *desire* is the fount from which fairy tales gush forth. There would, then, seem to be a connection between the fairy tales we write and the prayers we offer from the heart.

Clark believed that soul-sincere desires are implanted, molded and fashioned in us by the hand of God. One way to become aware of them is to go over the ambitions or fantasies we had during our childhood and adolescent years. A soul-sincere desire is no egocentric wish, according to Clark. Rather, it arises from the very center of our self. When realized, it will mutually benefit ourselves, society and those around us.

Spontaneous fairy tales may likewise give clues to our soul-sincere desires although couched in terms of image, symbol and story. Not only may they give us leads as to what is going on within us; but they offer, in their own way, an awareness of certain pitfalls facing us as well as the means by which to deal with them.

I offer this last observation with some reluctance, since the mere writing of the fairy tale is likely to be more significant than any subsequent analysis of it. Nevertheless, a week, a month, a year after writing your fairy tale, you might review it for motifs or themes, making associations of the images you find there and noting also the way by which the problem is resolved.

For example, the preacher, who could no longer sing, had lost something of real value—a certain form of harmony and self-expression. What this might mean to the man who wrote it, I do not know; but it speaks to me of a loss of spirit or *joi de vivre*. Nor does he get assistance from either the medical or common sense approach offered by his physician and his mother. Rather his interaction with his mother led to a bizarre remedy—the deep sea dive that restored him to health once again.

In the language of symbol, the preacher needs to get in

touch with the nurturing element of his soul (his mother) so he can go in depth to the restorative powers that lie within his own unconscious (the sea dive). It may well be he cannot do this if he maintains a rather frantic, busy and extroverted life which is causing a loss of spirit or an illness of the soul. He may need quiet-time for introversion, a retreat period. Like the prophet Jonah, this man may be running from an encounter and demand of God in which a meeting with the whale holds the potential for new life. Indeed, the writer of this tale might profit from reading this Old Testament Book and giving it his own interpretation.

The motif is highly Biblical. Like the sheep or coin in our Lord's parables, the issue is how to find again that which is lost. When it is found—the sheep, the coin, the voice—it will be experienced as finding energy; the restoration of wholeness and well-being; a fresh, revitalized relationship with God.

The tale of the discarded chair is reminiscent of the story, *The Velveteen Rabbit*. The rabbit likewise had been tossed aside after much use. But, like the stone the builders rejected that became the head stone (Luke 20:17, Acts 4:11), the chair became the most precious object in the house. Here something has not been lost but merely discounted and neglected. The story suggests that a quality, ability or attitude, once treasured, can be renewed and still contribute powerfully to the writer's life. What would the chair represent to the writer of the tale? And who is that person who affirms its worth?

Of course, my associations are mere speculations. The authors of the fairy tales are the final interpreters; the imagery, the symbols came out of them. Moreover, there is a real danger in writing fairy tales merely as an analytical tool because our egocentricity is likely to contaminate any story written with such a purpose in mind. Yet, despite the difficulties ego-manipulations would surely cause, fairy tales, when written spontaneously, do throw light on soul-sincere desires, the problems needing resolution, and the resources at hand through the providence of God.

The Transcendent Function

There are a multitude of definitions for spiritual direction. The one that I like is "freeing the soul for expansion and service." The director is a soul friend offering his / her support, prayers and insight as the directee seeks to discern God's will in his / her particular life.

In moments of crisis or in periods of "stuckness" the director might well suggest the writing of a fairy tale. Such an exercise is only one dimension of what C.G. Jung called the "transcendent function," the union of conscious and unconscious contents in active imagination.[28] Art, dance, other modes of story or drama, also unite the fantasy combinations of the unconscious with the ordered expression of consciousness.

The fairy tale that follows was written by a directee who was going through the trauma of vocational and marital disruption. The three chapters covered a time span of six to eight months. The story is incomplete. The directee has not fully worked through his problems. Nevertheless, the man was able to maintain a certain emotional balance in part through the vehicle of fairy tale—the creative use of his transcendent function.

A King's Search

CHAPTER I

Once upon a time there lived in a far country a mighty King who had conquered all his enemies. He had built himself a castle which dominated the countryside from where he governed his people with a just but iron hand.

You might think that such a King possessed all that his heart desired. He had wealth, power and honor, not to mention a young and healthy son.

However, such was not the case. Deep in the soul of the King there was a sorrow which as the years passed burdened him more and more. For his wife, the Queen, resented all that he had attained, the victories he won, the fame he possessed; and she despised her role as Queen.

Oh, there had been a period when the King ignored his wife's complaints and obvious depressions. Those were the days when there were battles being fought, the castle constructed and order brought into the land. Such pressing matters had turned the King's mind from the fact that the Queen's love had soured like poor wine. But the day came when the King could avoid the issue no longer. While peace prevailed in the countryside, within the castle the Queen sulked bitterly in her room.

At first the King tried to humor the Queen with parties, games and frivolity of every kind. He invited to his castle the finest artists and entertainers to perform before the Queen. It was to no avail. The Queen was disinterested with anything the King suggested. He pleaded with her to name that which would give her joy. Her only answer was that when he permitted her—the Queen—to rule in his stead, only then would she find again that love she once had for the King. But to allow the Queen to govern in his place was the one thing the King would not or could not do.

Finally, the King called a meeting of his wisest men and laid before them the problem he was suffering with the Queen. To exist without love, said the King to those gathered before him, was not to live at all.

Many suggestions were offered and weighed carefully by the King. He could banish his Queen from his castle and take another woman in her place; but because his son adored his mother, this the King refused to do.

He also might divide the land in two, permitting the Queen to rule over one part and himself the other; but this the King believed would lead to certain chaos, if not to war.

Or he could take another woman and have two Queens living in his castle, but the King was afraid that soon he would have two angry and bitter women rather than just one.

And finally he might abdicate his throne and turn the authority over to his son; but as the King concluded, this would, in fact, allow the Queen to govern through his son.

At last, the wisest of the wise, Harold the White, rose from his seat at Council and spoke his mind directly to his King. "Your Majesty," he began, "you have sought our advice, and we have offered it as best we can. I myself have argued that the shrewdest course would be to exile your Queen, who offers salt for sweetness and burs instead of flowers. But since you reject this, O King, I suggest another course. It is said that deep in the heart of the great forest resides an ancient woman, the Old Woman of the Wood, through whom the Divine speaks. According to the legends of the forest, she is dumb to all who demand an answer and do not know the sacred word. Be humble, my Lord. Seek out this Old Woman of the Wood, and perhaps this elder one will lift the stone that hangs so heavily on your soul."

That very night the King placed his castle in the hand of his most trusted Captain and set out to find the Old Woman of the Wood dressed as the commonest woodcutter in his realm.

Entering the great forest, the King discovered that beneath the canopy of boughs there was a honeycomb of many paths so that within moments the King had no idea which might lead him to the center of the Wood. The eerie rustling of the wind blowing through the trees was the only sound, as if the King were the only living creature in the forest.

Suddenly, an owl hooted, startling the King. And looking up, the King saw the bird fluttering its wings, hooting, flitting before him as if to guide him along the way.

"Better trust the owl," thought the King, "since I have no idea where I'm going." So the King followed the owl, moving in and out among the trees until they came to a clearing in what the King surmised must be the center of the forest. There in the open space was a small log hut, covered with a thatched roof.

The owl hooted and at the call, a huge wolf-dog appeared in the doorway and answered with a piercing howl. The wolf-dog sniffed the air and howled again, its glowing eyes penetrating the forest darkness so that the King knew he was spotted where he stood.

It was then that an old, old woman leaning on a gnarled staff showed herself at the cottage door and placed her other hand on the wolf-dog's shaggy mane. Beckoning, she indicated she saw as clearly as her dog the whereabouts of the wandering King.

As the King moved forward, the wolf-dog uttered a guttural growl. The old woman waited for him to speak.

"I am a troubled man," began the King, "I seek wisdom from the Old Woman of the Wood. I trust it is she to whom I speak. I would learn how to kindle the love of my wife to whom I have given all that is within my power, except the authority to rule in my own place."

The Old Woman did not reply, indeed she seemed hardly to have heard the words at all. And the King remembered that she was dumb to any who approached her too directly and did not possess the sacred word.

Then the Ancient One lifted her staff and revolved it in the air and then gestured with it, clearly dismissing the disappointed King. Rebuked, the King turned back to the great forest and wandered aimlessly in circles as if to fulfill the movement of the Old Woman's staff.

Days passed. The King lived on berries and struggled to maintain some hope. To his despair he neither saw nor heard any living creature, not even the distant hooting of the owl. Each morning when a faint glint of light shown through the blanket covering of trees, the King would rise, expecting that today he might stumble onto the clearing, or by some stroke of fortune get an inkling of the sacred word. Each night when darkness enveloped him again, he would fall exhausted beneath some giant tree and cry himself to sleep, for such was the state of mind of this once mighty King.

It was at such a moment, when the impenetrable darkness had settled for the night, that the King, lying by the trunk of a large tree, caught a murmur other than the wind blowing through the trees. It was the distant noise of rushing, ruffled water deep within the ground.

Feeling his way on hand and knee, the King moved slowly, seeking to catch the tiniest ebb and flow of sound. It was thus he literally fell into a cave which took him to a stairway leading down and down and down.

At last the earthen stairway ended and the King seemed to enter another land — a world of silvery moonlight in which objects could be distinguished while their features remained blurred. There before him rippling waters flowed and naked nymph-like women frolicked — swimming, laughing and cavorting in the stream. At the sight of the exhausted King they stopped their play and rushed to meet him as he collapsed beneath their feet. Soon their bodies brought him back to life and they joyfully ministered to his every need.

The time by the moonlit stream went by as quickly and as slowly as a dream.

It was the distant hooting of the owl that awoke the King from his trance-like state. "Fair damsels of the stream," cried the King, "can you tell me the sacred word that will release wisdom from the Old Woman of the Wood?"

As if they were a lovely chorus, the stream-nymphs replied, "Melody, Melody — the Old Woman vibrates to the harmony of sound." With this they left the King and splashing delightedly returned to their play within the stream.

Again it was the hooting owl who guided the King up the cavern stairs until once again he stood on firm forest ground. And following the bird moving in the trees, it was no time at all before the King stood in the clearing before the thatched hut guarded by the wolf-like hound.

The Old Woman stood at the door resting upon her gnarled cane while the wolf-dog snarled menacingly, showing his fanged teeth. However, the King approached with confidence and ease. Saluting the owl and the wolf-dog, the King called, "May Melody, Old Woman, fill your heart and all the woods!"

At the sound of the sacred word, the Old Woman lifted a small reed horn that hung beneath her neck and blew a note that awakened all the creatures of the woods. Instantly, the forest became alive with song. The wolf-dog lifted its head and howled in a way that blended with the symphony of sounds. And for the first time in years the King felt joy buoying up his heart.

After what seemed but a moment, the Old Woman of the Wood blew the note again. The music ceased as dramatically as it had begun.

"Welcome to my home," she told the King. "Enter, and we will speak of the concern that is on your heart." With that she led the King into her simple cottage with its dirt floor, and together they sat before a small hearth of burning coals while the wolf-dog lay with its head between its paws.

There was a long silence. Then the Old Woman looked directly at the King. "Your wife, the Queen, is sick with a malady that afflicts not only Woman but Man as well. We earthly creatures either bring music to another's soul, or seek to govern and control. We cannot have both. It is either/or—when you rule you cannot love; when you genuinely love, you seek not to rule. There was a time when your Queen played music on the harpstrings of your heart, those days before you became the mighty King. Only when she no longer brought you melody and song, did she seek to govern in your stead."

And taking the reed instrument from about her neck, the Old Woman gave it to the King. "Here is my horn. One note will cause all the people in your realm to sing, to experience the harmony of heaven within time. There is only one condition for its use. The horn will not sound unless the one who blows it is ruled by love more than the love of rule. Take it. Let your Queen taste melody again. Let her feel music welling up within her soul. Then offer her the choice—your Kingdom or my horn. Should she choose my gift, you will dance together on the throne. Should she elect the Kingdom, *you* will own the greatest treasure I can give."

"Suppose the horn will not sound when I put it to my lips," replied the King.

"That depends on the choice you will the Queen," answered the Old Woman smiling at the King.

The wolf-dog yawned and showed his fangs. The King arose clutching the horn, bowed to the Old Woman and walked out into the forest to seek his castle once again. And the owl hooted to show the King the way.

CHAPTER II

Scarcely had the King left the confines of the forest than he sensed something in the air. It was not long before he realized that the whole countryside was on the move, headed as was he in the direction of the castle.

Dressed as a woodcutter, the King had little fear of being recognized, so he approached a group resting by the road and asked where they were going.

"You have been in the woods a time," replied a man incredulously. "Haven't you heard, we crown the young lad King in the morning. We are all gathering to pay him homage as our rightful lord."

"How do you know the King is dead?" expostulated the King. "Why is this being done?"

Again the man reacted as though the King were a little mad. "Oh, woodcutter, you have been gone a spell. It is a year and a day since the King disappeared, saying he

115

would shortly return. Since then not a word has been heard. Better a boy-King ruled by his mother than uncertainty in the land. Already it is rumored that enemies are rising in the West."

Stunned by the news, the King sat down by a small river and looked at his image in the stream. It was not merely that a great beard covered his face. His whole countenance was altered, different from what he had been before. And the King realized, as he pondered his reflection, that part of him no longer desired to be King. He was seized by an overwhelming urge to disappear forever, become part of the multitude, or better still seek out a new identity in another land.

"I *have* changed," thought the King. "Perhaps I am no longer fit to rule. But I have the horn," he mused. On impulse he put the horn to his lips and blew. The effect was instantaneous! It was as if the earth stood up to sing. The cattle mooed, the donkeys brayed, the dogs howled, the birds burst forth in melodious song, while the people on the road danced as if moving to a divine and inner tune.

Again the King sounded the horn. A hush fell over the land, but joy filled the King's heart as well as those around him. His depression lifted, the King joined the crowd now gaily climbing towards the castle. However, the closer he drew to his home the more unsure the King became as to what he now should do. For if he revealed his identity before he talked with the Queen, it would make it difficult for the Queen to make the free choice prescribed by the Old Woman of the Wood.

So it was that a startled guard was asked for an audience with the Queen by a woodcutter with a shaggy beard. Taking a ring from his finger, the disguised King assured the hesitant man that at one glance the Queen would wish to see him. It was not long thereafter that the King and the Queen met privately the night before the crowning of their son.

"It *is* you," gasped the Queen. And then with tears in her eyes and reproach in her voice she asked, "Why did you leave me without a word; why did you let us sorrow and grieve? Why do you return now?"

116

The King took the Queen's hands in his own and looked deeply into her eyes. "I didn't realize I had been gone so long," he began. "I was seeking a way to rekindle our love with the help of the Old Woman of the Wood." And as best he could, the King told his wife his tale.

"By the river I blew the horn," continued the King. "I didn't know whether it would sound for me."

"I felt melody in my heart," sighed the Queen. "For the first time in many a year there was music in my soul."

"You have your choice," the King said slowly. "You can choose to govern the land through our son, or accept this gift which causes life to sing." And taking the horn in his two hands, the King offered it to the Queen.

There was a long silence. The Queen looked steadily at the King, and again tears streamed down from her eyes. Then she drew herself up to her full height, and her eyes blazed.

"You speak of the choice that is given *me*, but what about the one that is offered *you*? You wish me to take the horn so that we can dance together on the throne. But what if I choose to govern, leaving you the horn? The decision is then yours, not mine. For years you neglected me, while you grew to be the mighty King. You blame me for the souring of our love as though the fault were mine. I sought the intimacy of your heart. Gone were the times when I shared the burdens of your soul. You only asked that I fulfill the outward functions of your Queen. You cared less and less for me—more and more for power and for rule. Oh, my husband, if choice is what you ask, I would choose closeness and love with you. But if you have not this to give, I choose to rule the land through the person of our son. And even then, if you wish to stay and use your horn, the land will sing and our son reign well. My King, the choice is yours."

A great sadness fell between them. The King's eyes glistened, whether from disappointment in himself or his wife, he did not know.

"I no longer need to rule," he murmured, "but I believe it is what I am called to do. You are right, we both have need to choose. I will be going to start my life anew. But if you or my son have need of me, I will return. And you both will be treasured in my heart."

117

In the early dawn before the crowning of the child as King, a woodcutter left the castle and began a lonely journey down the circuitous road from the castle to the rolling plains where roads crossed, leading east and west, north and south. Each one led to another land where life might begin again.

The woodcutter had asked one last favor of his Queen —that she would give the horn from the Old Woman of the Wood as a coronation gift to their young son. "Who knows," thought the King, "he may be the one to rise in power and blow the horn as well."

CHAPTER III

Before the King lay four choices. He could start his quest by turning east or west, south or north. Each direction led to a Kingdom over which he had no control, with no status or identity.

To the east lay the Kingdom of the First-Born. In it the eldest of any family, male or female, ruled. It was a land of law and order, the acceptance of fixed rules.

To the north lay the Kingdom of Light and Darkness. For a time the just would govern, only to be overthrown by the powers of evil and tyranny. The good would then regain control and the cycle would begin again.

Toward the south was the country of Magician's Charm. It was said that once you entered this realm, you were caught in a fantasy and dream from which you might never return.

And to the west was the Kingdom of the Great Unknown. Indeed, no one had ever gone there or come from there as far as the King knew. Yet time and again rumors went abroad that threatening forces were rising in the west, dangers which had never materialized over the years.

Perplexed, the King sat by the crossroad on a large stone, wishing for the friendly owl who had helped him in the woods. But when no owl appeared, he just sat there with his head on his hands, reflecting upon his state. Should he have renounced the throne, he wondered. Regrets, recriminations began to fill his heart. After all, he was the King. Should he have offered the horn to his young son? Perhaps the horn would assist him now in some mysterious way.

Scarcely had this thought passed through his mind than the whole creation began to sing and the King felt melody playing in his soul, such that he leaped up to dance and sing. There was no doubt. His young son had blown the horn to bring joy to his coronation day.

In that moment, hope revived the King. He arose and turned to the west, setting forth towards the land of the Great Unknown.

After several days the King realized that no landmarks seemed familiar. The road he had been following narrowed to a path and then came to an abrupt end. The King found himself in a country of flowing streams and lovely trees as he made his way over terrain which, as far as he could see, had never been traversed before.

The countryside was hilly. The King became aware that, imperceptibly, he had been climbing for some time. Suddenly, as he reached the crest of a steep slope, the King saw before him the loveliest city he had ever seen, nestling in a valley below. It was a city, he later discovered, that glowed not only in the sunlight, but in the moonlight as well. As the King approached, he heard birds singing as if responding to the Old Woman's horn. And it was not long before the tired King found himself among warmhearted people with smiling faces, people who spoke a language as lilting and melodious as the birds warbling in the trees. They welcomed the stranger without surprise, sat him down in an outdoor inn, and offered him food and drink.

When the King had eaten his fill, a man approached him, bowed with respect and beckoned the King to follow. Soon they were ushered into a home where women and children were laughing as they worked at a variety of tasks, all the while keeping up animated conversations. One of the women came forward. She took his hands in hers and warmly greeted him in her foreign tongue. When her blue eyes met the King's it was as though a wave of energy coursed through his whole body. He had never met anyone who had touched him so vibrantly before. Smiling, the woman took him by the hand and led him into another room where a tall man arose to meet him.

"I am called 'Innocent,'" he began, "not because I am so naive, but because of what I have become. You have met my wife, Adriane, I see. We have been expecting for some time a stranger from the east. When the horn blows in your country it means that someone will be drawn to our land. Please be seated. You will have an opportunity later to speak at length with Adriane."

"You are kind to welcome a foreigner," replied the King. "Perhaps you wish to hear my story or let me tell you who I am."

"Your past is not our concern." Innocent dismissed the overture with a wave of his hand. "This is the land of possibility, of what will be and what you will become. Our pasts have brought us here, but are of interest to ourselves alone."

"Then hear my desire." continued the King. "I seek to begin anew. What must I do to find a place among your people, who seem so gracious and so kind?"

"It is not a matter of doing but of being," answered Innocent. "In the beginning we ask a stranger merely to be with us, to disclose whatever is passing through his mind, to share his visions and his hopes, to discuss openly his ideas, to challenge and be challenged in the spirit of forbearance and of love. You see, this is a land where relationships count more than achievements; where the power to sustain community is valued; and power over others is a sign of weakness rather than of strength."

"I have been feeling guilty and not a little angry with myself," confessed the King, "for abdicating my power and giving to others the responsibilities that were mine to bear. Are you saying that in this country what I did might be correct?"

"No," replied Innocent reflectively, "abdication of responsibility is the other side of tyranny. We desire that you be accountable for your life, do your work and bear your share. Rather, we find people far more conscious in what they do if they test their ideas and talk about their feelings before they undertake the tasks they have in mind. Only then are we ready to place our mark upon the world. This means a discipline of sorts. We take time for one another here."

There was much more to say. But in the ensuing weeks and months the King experienced the truth of all that Innocent had told him. Never was the King alone if he cherished companionship. Never was he pressed to be other than himself. And when in fantasy he considered standing up and crying, "Hear, one and all, that I am a King," he realized they would respond in kind, "And so are we all in this fair land."

Never had the King tested his ideas with such sharp minds, nor expressed his feelings with persons who so accepted and understood them. Not just men, but women sat with him for hours to listen and respond to what he had to say. And for the first time the King heard others in return. Yet the effort to stay in dialogue with others until a matter had been worked through, was one which tried his soul. However, it was with Adriane that the King discovered a whole new meaning in his life. A woman of rare charm, Adriane seemed to draw out of him the very center of his being. With her he felt that he was someone who was important for himself and not as King. Her insights often took him by surprise, for she was in touch with truths of her own being in ways that overwhelmed him.

As the days passed, the King fell more and more in love with Adriane—a situation which they shared completely, treasured on both sides. One day the King blurted forth, "Adriane, my darling, you are my Queen!" And Adriane nodded and replied, "I know."

"But what of Innocent?" cried out the King in agony.

"He is still my husband," answered Adriane, "but he has never been my soul."

It was not long after this exchange that the King's routine was shattered by an unexpected event. To his surprise, one morning Innocent came to him with news. "We have word," he said, "that trouble is brewing in your land. The horn blows with no response. The birds tell us that evil rides the air. What you will do, I do not presume to guess; but it is important that you know."

If such tidings had arrived months earlier, the King might have rejoiced at the opportunity to return. But now things were different. His love for Adriane possessed him. There was hardly a minute when she did not dominate his mind. He could not remember a time in recent weeks when there had been any desire on his part to reign again. Nevertheless, he had promised the Queen that he would come back if needed, and deep within he felt the call to aid his struggling son. But his last moments with Adriane tore to shreds the feelings of his heart.

"Adriane, my darling, I love as I have never loved before. I will come back to you when this battle has been won."

Adriane could hardly speak, so violent were her tears. "My beloved," she said, "you will be with me in spirit till you return."

It was several days and nights before the King came once again in sight of his castle fortress silhouetted against the sky. There was little doubt that evil was abroad. Gangs of men stopped him, searched him, or gave him dark and questioning stares. Any stranger was not welcome. Suspicion stood sentinel in every mind. In the end, the King would not have been permitted within the walls if he had not again demanded of a guard that the Queen see the ring that he presented. This talisman quickly brought a messenger. And again the King was ushered into a room where he and his Queen might be alone.

The Queen looked haggard. Her face was drawn and hard. The King was shocked at how much she seemed to have aged.

"I might have known it was you that was stirring up the people!" began the Queen. But in the next moment she broke into choking sobs. The King gathered her into his arms and held her tightly. "Do not be afraid," he said,

"I have returned as I promised. It is not too late. All will be well."

"It is your old captains that have risen in revolt," bitterly exclaimed the Queen. "They never accepted me nor the rule of our young son. And then the horn no longer blew." Her voice trailed off.

"You forget," the King said softly, "that the horn blows only for those who rule by love, and not by those who love to rule."

At this the Queen burst into tears, sobbing wretchedly. "I wanted to rule—to show you, if no one else, that I could govern as well as you. I wanted to rule because you cast me away from your heart, the deepest kind of wound."

The King took the Queen by her hands and looked into her eyes. "I was wrong leaving you both the way I did, but then I did not have the knowledge I have now. But before war breaks out and our castle is beseiged, I plead with you to call the people and announce that I have returned to act as Regent for our son. When he has matured, I will step aside to let him reign."

So it was that the King returned. The people cheered and cheered, and when his son handed him the horn, melody filled the land.

"But the day the horn blows again from my son's lips," mused the King, "I will return to Adriane."

To Be Continued

■ ■ ■

Additional Comments

There the tale hangs suspended. The King has not resolved his relationship with his Queen nor with Adriane. His role in the world remains uncertain.

It would have been tempting for the spiritual director to have stepped in after the first or second chapter to make some analytical comment. Fortunately, he did not. He allowed the directee to play with his story freely, choosing his material from where he willed like a child in a sandbox.

Therapeutically, many questions could be raised about the directee's relationship to his feminine side, and his use of personal power. It is significant that his central figure is a "King." But such insights prematurely raised may abort the process. The objectifying and telling of the story is healing in itself.

The tale needs to be completed before such issues may be raised.

Active Imagination
and the Bible

One of the positive side effects of writing your own fairy tales is your increased ability to use active imagination with Holy Scripture. In his little book, *The Bible in Human Transformation*, Walter Wink notes that we need not only the insight and understanding which comes by reading and encountering the Biblical word but "the truth of our own personal and social being as it is laid bare by dialectical interpretation of the text."[29] For example, after examining the healing of the paralytic (Matthew 9:1-8, Mark 2:1-12, Luke 5:17-26), comparing the three accounts, putting the stories in their social / historical context and in the perspective of the particular Gospel, further questions can be asked. Who is the paralytic in you? What aspect of your life is unable to function? Who is the scribe in you? What part of me is always judging me and making me feel unworthy? Who are the helpers? What resources can move my paralytic side to the healing source? And finally, how does Christ speak to the paralytic, the scribes, the helpers in me?

One way to discover how these figures in you react is to write out your own scenario and let them speak to one another. The same transcendent function exercised in your fairy tale will be released, in this case tapping the well of your religious faith.

The problem of so much Biblical study, according to Wink, is that the student is not touched at depth by his / her effort. In the parable of the Pharisee and tax collector (Luke

18:9-14), any reader knows that the Pharisees are hypocrites and the publican is closer to the Kingdom with his outburst, "God be merciful to me a sinner!" Any modern student will identify with the tax collector as the good guy. Hence, the story is deformed into one teaching cheap grace; i.e., Jesus justified the sinner because he recognized his sin and asked for mercy. However, it is *Jesus* who declares the tax collector right before God and not the tax collector himself; the tax collector does not know he is forgiven unless he encounters Jesus for himself. Nor has the Pharisee been enabled to change. Transformation does not take place in the reader until his guilty, sinful side engages in dialogue with the self-righteous Pharisee in him/her and the two of them with Christ. A similar critique, but somewhat differently approached, is offered by Karl A. Olsson in his two books *Find Your Self in the Bible* and *Meet Me on the Patio*.[30] Olsson's "relational Bible studies" call for people to identify with a character in a Biblical story and in the situation which the narrative describes. Both Olsson and Wink are advocates of group Bible study in a personal and imaginative fashion.

Parables, also, make excellent food for this kind of process, since they are already expressing the dynamics of the Kingdom. For example, in the parable of the Prodigal Son, the story ends with the elder son still outside the home in which the Prodigal is enjoying the celebration. In a sense, it is incomplete. The reconciliation between the two brothers, the Father's great concern, has not taken place. Why not then have the Prodigal Son go out to talk with his brother and write your dialogue with the same prayerful relish and spontaneity that you did with your fairy tale? How it should take place for you I have no idea, but here is mine for what it is worth:

P for Prodigal: "Brother, I don't blame you for being angry with me or Dad, but for his sake and not mine, come on in and join the party."

E for Elder Brother: "You s.o.b., I wouldn't celebrate your return after what you did to embarrass our family unless you were brought home in a casket."

P: "Listen, we are brothers and we were friends once.

Forgive me. I can't tell you how sorry and wretched I feel. How can I enjoy anything until you pardon me also?

E: "It's incredible to me how Dad could have let you off so easy. First he gave you the money, which was unbelievable in itself, and then he welcomes you back as though you were some kind of hero instead of a fast-talking con artist. No, I won't give you anything, even if our Father has lost his head."

P: "You may not know how it feels to be in another country with no money, feeding pigs, and a conscience that won't let you go. That's where I've been, brother. It's what I deserved; I had it coming. You may not believe this, but I came back to be a hired hand."

E: "You came back because you can talk Father into anything. Look at you, a ring on your finger, shoes on your feet, the best calf killed in your honor. No one ever did that for me."

P: "Father did that. I can't understand it either. I guess he was just plain glad to see me. I'm sure he thought I was dead."

E: "Frankly, I wish you were. I wish that you had never returned and all this hadn't happened. I'm so shocked by what Father has done. I don't know if I can ever have the same relationship with him again."

P: "It's changed as far as I'm concerned. I'll never take advantage of him again."

E: "So you say now. But wait. You'll probably run off again and the same thing will happen all over again."

P: "Didn't you ever worry about me, brother? Didn't you ever want me back? We were friends as well as brothers once."

E: "I did. I prayed you'd return safely. That you'd learn your lesson. But I thought Father would at least like me more than you because I stayed home and did the work for both of us."

P: "Are you more angry with Dad than you are with me?"

E: "I am. By God, I am."

P: "Brother, for my sake then, come in and join me. I

can't take Dad's love without you. It will kill me. Brother, believe me, I can't accept it without you."
E: "I will go on one condition. That you do nothing when I tell Father what I think of him and you in front of everyone."

■ ■ ■

Or suppose you were one of those wicked tenants that rented the landowner's farm and then refused to pay the rent, killing and driving the owner's employees away and then killing his son so they could have the land for themselves. That we treat the Kingdom of God within us like an absentee landlord may not sound rational, but it may be unpleasantly true. So you be the Renter and let God send first an employee and then his son:

R for Renter: "And who are you, trespassing on my property?"
E for Employee: "I'm from your Landlord. It's time to collect the rent."
R: "You get out of here. I've done all the work. The fruits are mine. The money is mine. If it weren't for me there would be no farm."
E: "Listen, he set you up. He bought the farm, planted the vineyards. You had nothing. He gave you everything."
R: "Big deal. That Master of yours owns the whole world. He won't miss anything I withhold from him, and since I've been using what he left me, it's mine. Possession's nine-tenths of the law."
E: "The fact is, you don't own the property; and, frankly, what he's asking is really very little in my opinion. Just a portion for himself."
R: "You get the hell out of here. I don't need your Master anymore. I don't want you or him around my place and I'm not giving one penny of my hard-earned money back. You hear?"
Enter Jesus Christ.
J.C.: "I'm the Master's son. I'm here to visit his property and collect the rent."
R: "Oh, so you're the son. And just how do I know that?"

J.C.: "You know it because you feel the same in my presence as you did in his."

R: "That doesn't prove a thing. You get off my land or I'll do to you what I did to all those other servants that claimed to be from your Master, or whatever his name is."

J.C.: "Why are you unwilling to admit he gave you everything you have or own? Why are you so ungrateful and so frightened to have me in your home?"

R: "I like it just the way it is. I owe no one anything. I can do what I want. And all that I make is mine—MINE."

J.C.: "Look, my Father doesn't hate you. He loves you. He doesn't need your money, but you need to give it, or you'll never know his love, nor will anyone living around you. It's you who needs to give. It's you who needs him."

R: "That's a lot of blarney, I don't need him anymore. I don't need you or anyone else, for that matter. And what I do need I can buy myself, and then others need to deal with me. That's the law of living—get others dependent on you."

J.C.: "Well, since this is my Father's property, I'm staying."

R: "Listen, buddy, you try to stay on my land or in my house, I'll kill you."

J.C.: "And I'll keep coming back."

R: "The hell you will . . . ."

■ ■ ■

Here then is the other advantage of writing your own fairy tales. You learn an art by which Scripture can come alive as you enter into the story and make it your own through fantasy.

It may have been that in oral and more unsophisticated periods of history, just hearing the story as God's Word was sufficient to transform the hearer. However, today you need a technique to experience the reality of the Kingdom as the scriptural Word addresses you. The Kingdom of God is

129

no fairy tale. But you can enrich your understanding of it if you use the method of fairy tale to encounter its depths within you.

What is important, of course, is not that you agree with any particular insights and correlations in this book, but that you discover the presence of the Kingdom of God for yourself and have the experience of writing your own fairy tales. The discovery of the Kingdom of God entails a change of heart, mind and attitude. It is right here. Once we uncover it, once we are aware of it, we are never the same.

Repentance and love open our eyes to the Reality and presence of the Kingdom. Commitment and perseverance enable us to realize it. This is the message of the New Testament and fairy tales as well. We are called into a quest in which we will face trials—almost insurmountable difficulties. But with Providence and faith, we can come through darkness to the light on the other side. Moreover, fairy tales emphasize another aspect of the Gospel that sometimes is lost. Growing in the Kingdom does not protect us from pain and suffering, although it does open us up to joy. Holiness, or wholeness, comes through a journey, a quest, a pilgrimage that takes place as much within as without. The road may be rocky, while dangers lurk in dark places. As such, our life in Christ is often a wounding that we may be healed, a smiting that we may find peace, a dying that we may be raised up.

As a companion on the Way, I wish you well. Pray for me as a sinner.

Notes

1. J. R. R. Tolkien, *Tree and Leaf,* Boston, Houghton Mifflin Co., 1965, p. 72.
2. T. S. Eliot, "East Coker," *Four Quartets,* New York, Harcourt, Brace and Co., 1943, p. 14.
3. Rosemary Haughton, *Tales from Eternity,* New York, Seabury Press, 1973, p. 39.
4. Quoted on p. 2 of *The Secular Meaning of the Gospel* by Paul Van Buren, New York and London, The MacMillan Co., 1963.
5. C. S. Lewis, *The Magicians's Nephew,* New York, Macmillan Publishing Co., Inc., 1970, p. 107.
6. John A. Sanford, *The Kingdom Within,* Philadelphia, J.B. Lippincott Company, 1970, p.117.
7. J. R. R. Tolkien, *The Fellowship of the Ring,* New York, Ballantine Books, 1965, p.110.
8. William Temple, *Readings in St. John's Gospel,* London, MacMillan and Co., Ltd., 1952, p.226.
9. J. R. R. Tolkien, *The Return of the King,* New York, Ballantine Books, 1965, p. 140.
10. J. R. R. Tolkien, *The Two Towers,* New York, Ballantine Books, 1965, pp. 234-235.
11. J. R. R. Tolkien, *The Fellowship of the Ring, op. cit.,* p.7.
12. Arthur Cochrane, " Barmen Revisited," *Christianity and Crisis,* Vol. 33, No. 22, December 24, 1973, pp. 267-269.
13. J. R. R. Tolkien, *The Fellowship of the Ring, op. cit.,* pp. 514-515.
14. *Ibid.,* pp.429-430.
15. *Ibid.,* p. 354.
16. *Ibid.,* p. 403.
17. J. R. R. Tolkien, *The Return of the King, op. cit.,* p. 274.
18. Unpublished paper from Apple Farm group discussions, February 1968, pp. 10-11. Reprinted with permission.
19. C. S. Lewis, *Surprised by Joy,* New York, Harcourt, Brace and Co., 1956, p. 228.
20. Gert Behanna: pseudonym of Elizabeth Burns, well-known speaker and writer who wrote her autobiography of an ex-pagan under the title, *The Late Liz* (New York, Appleton-Century, 1957).
21. J. R. R. Tolkien, *The Fellowship of the Ring, op. cit.,* p. 95.
22. C. S. Lewis, *The Voyage of the Dawntreader,* New York, Macmillan Publishing Co., Inc., 1970, p. 215.
23. C. S. Lewis, *The Lion, the Witch and the Wardrobe,* New York, Macmillan Publishing Co., Inc., 1970, pp. 149-152.

24. C. S. Lewis, *The Voyage of the Dawntreader, op. cit.,* pp. 88-91.

25. *Ibid.,* p. 92.

26. C. S. Lewis, *The Last Battle,* New York, Macmillan Publishing Co., Inc., 1970, p. 146.

27. Glenn Clark, *I Will Lift Up My Eyes,* New York, Harper & Row, 1937, p. 44.

28. C. G. Jung, *The Transcendent Function,* Zurich, privately printed for the Students' Association, C. G. Jung Institute, 1957.

29. Walter Wink, *The Bible in Human Transformation,* Philadelphia, Fortress Press, 1973, p. 64.

30. Karl A. Olsson, *Find Your Self in the Bible* and *Meet Me on the Patio,* Minneapolis, Augsburg Publishing House, 1974 and 1977.